MESSENGERS
OF
MESSIAH

WITNESSING ENCOUNTERS
WITH THE CHOSEN PEOPLE

FOREWORD BY ZOLA LEVITT

TODD BAKER PH.D.

Copyright © 2006 by Dr. Todd Damon Baker
1st Printing

Messengers of Messiah
by Todd Baker, Ph.D.

Printed in the United States of America

ISBN 1-60034-398-8

All rights reserved solely by the author. The author guarantees all contents are original and do not infringe upon the
legal rights of any other person or work. No part of this book
may be reproduced in any form without the permission of
the author. The views expressed in this book are not neces-
sarily those of the publisher.

Unless otherwise indicated, Bible quotations are taken from
the New King James Version. Copyright © 1985 by Moody
Press.

The book was assembled using Adobe Pagemaker 7.0.

For further information, please contact the author:

Dr. Todd Damon Baker
Email: toddbus@yahoo.com

www.xulonpress.com

"For I am not ashamed of the gospel of Christ, for it is the power of God to salvation for everyone who believes, for the Jew first and also for the Greek."

Romans 1:16

Contents

Foreword

Inexplicably, especially in these End Times, there are few missionaries who venture to Israel. Christians **willingly travel to the remotest and most inhospitable parts of the earth, seeking those with whom they may share God's Good News.** But the one unique people in history to already believe in Him and the Old Testament are regularly ignored and left without the Gospel, the perfect completion of Judaism, being taught and explained to them. The majority of missionaries who do end up traveling to Israel seek converts among the Arabs in God's land, which is indeed a noble thing, and often a dangerous one. But within Christendom there is a bias away from presenting the Jews with the message Jesus Himself brought to them 2,000 years ago in order that *they* would end up telling *the world*!

This ongoing circumvention of God's Chosen People by the Church violates the latter part of Romans 1:16, and exists for a variety of reasons, not the least of which is anti-Semitism. As in the unbelieving world, anti-Semitism in Christendom is sadly not limited to the past one hundred years, nor to Americans alone. It has for centuries been weaved into the doctrines of such

European main-line denominations as the Roman Catholic Church, and many Protestant churches as well.

This history of hate toward them is a chief reason why modern Jews are generally not copasetic with Christianity. Indeed, they are taught to view Christ and Christians as the antitheses of being Jewish – this is an irony only the devil could cook up. Satan has always sought to drive a wedge between the Chosen People and their Saving Grace, as well as those who would be their brothers in Christ – Jewish and Gentile Christians. This is why we Believers must be proactive in bringing the Chosen to the truth of their Savior's act of salvation.

To fill this need, there is a fund in place, "To the Jew First" (Rom. 1:16), through our ministry which sends missionaries, like Dr. Todd Baker, to specifically target Jewish areas largely neglected by the universal Gospel outreach. In their periodic travels throughout Israel, these **Messengers of Messiah** have found a great number of soft hearts which have been divinely ripened for God's truth, not just among the Jews, but among Arabs and other people to whom the Lord has led them. Dr. Baker has had a call on his life for over 20 years to take our very Jewish Messiah back to those who first gave Him to us. Our Lord's Second Coming is imminent, and this evangelistic effort fulfills a call similar to that of John the Baptist to his *Jewish* brethren, ***"Prepare ye the way of the Lord, make his paths straight"*** *(Matt 3:3).*

Zola Levitt

2006

Introduction

Twenty-two years ago, I was a bellicose, drug-abusing atheist who had a passion for hating Christians and anyone else who claimed to believe in God. I studied the works of German philosopher Friedrich Nietzsche (1844 -1900) and other authors of atheism and blasphemy who could feed and justify the hate in my soul. In my descending darkness and destitution, the Lord Jesus appeared to me.

The piercing light of His Glory filled my room one late night in April of 1984. He identified Himself as "Jesus Christ, Whom you have persecuted!" I was brought out of the pit and radically changed that night. But not just for the sake of my soul. He commissioned me in ministry to His people. I soon learned that He was preparing me from the very pages of Scripture to proclaim to the people of Abraham, Isaac, and Jacob the return of the One whom they have pierced (Zechariah 12:10).

There have been many years of preparation for this ministry and this book chronicles the realization of that preeminent call.

As my partners and I travel to Israel to bring the message of Messiah to the Chosen people, we are in awe and humbly amazed at what God is doing, one on one with those whom His heart desires. We are convinced through the Word of God that this is an end time ministry, preparing the way for the Lord's return.

As you read through these pages, you will see that it doesn't read like an ordinary book. We pray without ceasing for months in advance of these trips. Our dialogue is genuine and unique to each individual through the inspiration of the Holy Spirit. I believe that God has required me to thoroughly document these conversations so that any who read this book can be enlightened to the truth about His desired solidarity between the Messiah, the Jewish people and the church. To that end this book makes a great unobtrusive witnessing tool for Jewish friends and neighbors.

It is my sincere hope that the readers of this book will be provoked to love, prayer, and support for the Jewish people and to the ministries that have been ordained by God to bring the Gospel of Christ Jesus our Lord back to the people of His origin.

Acknowledgments

The author would like to make the following acknowledgements:
- To all those who donate to this ministry
- To my fellow co-laborers in Christ who greatly helped me on these trips—Kevin Parker, Robert Cuccia, and Paul Colley.
- To Shalom, Shalom Messianic Congregation in Dallas, Texas, for their prayers and support.
- To Mark and Sandra Levitt for their ongoing support and belief in this vital ministry.
- To Teresa Brown for her continual assistance and encouragement of this project.
- To Bethsaida Messianic congregation in Haifa, Israel, for opening up their fellowship to these wayfarers in Israel.
- To Aaron Levarko and the staff of *Immanuel Bookshop* in Jerusalem for supplying us with Hebrew New Testaments and spiritual edification along the way.
- To Eric Morey of *The Galilee Experience* in Tiberius, Israel, for his faithful provision of Gospel tracts and Hebrew Bibles.
- To Elisa Retzlaff for her creative genius on formatting the newsletter and this book from which the newsletters come.

All of you have made it possible for us to bring Yeshua the Messiah back to the land and people He uniquely loves—the land of Israel and the Jewish people. ✡✝✡

This book is respectfully dedicated to the ministry and memory of Zola Levitt who was a dear friend, co-worker in Christ, and spiritual mentor. I am indebted to Zola for giving me the wonderful opportunity to repeatedly travel to Israel and witness to the Jewish people about their Messiah.

In loving memory of
Zola Levitt
1938 - 2006

Chapter 1:
Seven Reasons From Scripture Why the Gospel Must Go To the Jewish People

Brit Hadashah Ministries is committed to proclaiming the Gospel to the Jewish people in Israel. I have conducted several Gospel outreaches in Israel. We found the Jewish people there to be open, appreciative, and interested in the good news of Jesus the Messiah. Several individuals there have accepted Him as their Lord and Savior and became completed Jews born anew in the Messiah. Taking the Gospel to the Jews of Israel is not an option or choice for us, it is commanded by God in Scripture. In fact the Bible provides seven reasons why this is so. Seven, in the Bible, is the number of divine completeness. God created and completed the universe in seven days. Christ spoke seven times from the cross when completing the work of redemption. Seven years are left of Daniel's 70 weeks to complete the present age with the return of Christ to earth. And here God gives seven reasons for preaching the Gospel to Israel. Let's look at them in closer detail.

1 ***Romans 1:16* plainly says the Gospel is to go to the Jew first.** Paul writes in that passage: ***"For I am not ashamed of the Gospel of Christ, for it is the power of God to salvation to the Jew first and also to the Gentile."*** Here we have the divine order of evangelism defined. The Gospel is to go to the Jew first. Why? The answer is not because the Jewish people are somehow superior to the rest of the Gentile world, but because God chose their nation and people through whom the Messiah would come. He prepared them for this through the Covenants, the Hebrew Scriptures with its many Messianic prophecies, and the Temple and its sacrifices (see *Romans 15:8-9* where the divine order of evangelism is confirmed again). Thus Jesus came to save the Jews as a Jew. Jesus came first to offer salvation and the Messianic kingdom to Israel. He said as much during His ministry on earth. When sought by a Gentile, Jesus said in *Matthew 15:24*: ***"I am not sent but to the lost sheep of the House of Israel."*** Paul and the Apostles followed this divine order in the book of Acts when going to the Jews in the synagogues to preach the Gospel. Salvation and the Messiah came directly from the Jewish people. Jesus told the Samaritan woman in *John 4:22*: *"Salvation is of the Jews."* The Church is to follow the same order of evangelism given in *Romans 1:16* as practiced by the Lord Jesus and the Apostles. We are to witness to the Jews first as they did and commanded us to do.

2 **The Great Commission was given from Jerusalem and the preaching of the Gospel began there**. The holy city of Jerusalem is mentioned 811 times in Scripture. God has chosen this city as the eternal city where He will place His name forever (*2 Chron. 6:6*). Jesus will reign over the world from Jerusalem for a thousand years. Ezekiel 5:5 says God has placed Jerusalem at the center of the earth. There our Lord died for the sins of the world and was raised again. He will return there when He comes again. In *Acts 1:8*, Christ commanded the Disciples to take the Gospel to the whole world starting in Jerusalem. Jerusalem has been the Jewish capital for 3,000 years. It is not only logical but also strategically smart that if one preaches the Gospel to the Jews, you should go to the place they hold highest above all else on earth—Jerusalem.

3 **To fulfill prophecy and hasten the return of the Lord Jesus Christ.** There is an obscure and often ignored prophecy found in *Matthew 10:23*. Jesus said there *"But when they persecute you in this city, flee to another. For assuredly, I say to you, you will not have gone through the cities of Israel before the Son of Man comes."* Jesus predicted in this prophecy that the evangelization of the cities of Israel will not be complete before He returns. This prophecy will be fulfilled during the time of the tribulation period when Jewish Christians are persecuted for their Gospel witness in Israel. For nearly 2,000 years of the present Church age, the Gospel was not being preached to Jews in Israel because they were scattered throughout the nations of the world since

70 A.D. But all that changed in 1948 when Israel became a nation again and Jews returned en masse to their ancient homeland.

The Messianic movement in Israel is growing and now, for the first time since the days of Jesus and the Apostles, evangelism and gospel preaching to the Jews is happening in the land again. The fact that this has started and will not be finished before the Second Coming must mean the Lord's return is very soon. Not only do we have a prophecy of this kind found in the New Testament but also one of similar fashion in the Old Testament. It is in *Isaiah 62:10-12. Isaiah 62:10-12* is an amazing prophecy that says God will send Gentile believers to Jerusalem *"from the ends of the earth"* to proclaim to the Jewish inhabitants of Jerusalem that the Savior is coming to redeem and rescue them. Incidentally, the Hebrew word for "salvation" in *Isaiah 62:11* is the same word for the name of Jesus in Hebrew— Yeshua or Yeshuach. Yeshua (Jesus in English) means "The Lord is salvation." ***"She shall bear a Son, and you shall call His name Jesus (Yeshua)"*** (*Matthew 1:21*). ***"For He shall save His people from their sins."*** In other words, God wants them to say to Jerusalem "Yeshua (or Jesus) is coming!"

The chapter closes with the prediction that these Gentile ambassadors of Christ will prepare the way for the return of Yeshua the Savior in much the same way John the Baptist prepared Israel for the Messiah's first coming as predicted in *Isaiah 40:3*. This interpretation is confirmed by the fact that *Isaiah 63* opens with the second coming of the Messiah in glory after His way has been prepared by His Gentile ambassadors of chapter 62 who come to share the Gospel of salvation to Israel and Jerusalem. The fact that this ministry and others are doing this very thing means prophecy is being fulfilled and Christ's coming is extremely close.

4 **Preaching the Gospel to Israel pays the debt we Gentile believers owe to the Jewish people.** Paul said in *Romans 15:27* that we are indebted to Israel because of the spiritual blessings they brought to the world. Those blessings that came through the Jewish people are the Bible, the Messiah, and the Judeo-Christian ethic on which the whole of Western civilization is built. The New Testament Church is obligated out of Christ's love to share the Gospel to His ethnic people—the Jews. What greater way to pay that spiritual debt of gratitude than to share with them the great riches of salvation given through Jesus Christ.

5 **To prepare Jewish hearts for the Tribulation.** The signs of the Lord's return are here to anybody who has a basic understanding of Bible prophecy. When you witness to an Israeli Jew in this late hour, you could very well be planting Gospel seed that will save him after the Rapture and allow him to become part of the 144,000 Jewish evangelists mentioned in Revelation 7. God's Word will not return void. Jews we witness to now who do not get saved can still have a chance, after the Rapture of the Church, when they recall what we told them about this event and the tribulation period to follow.

6 **The Salvation of Israel is the heart cry of God and Jesus.** Our Lord wept over the lost condition of Jerusalem saying, *"O Jerusalem, Jerusalem, the one who kills the prophets and stones those who are sent to her! How often I wanted to gather your children together, as a hen gathers her chicks under her wings, but you were not willing"* (*Matthew 23:37*). Jesus lamented over the fact that they would reject Him as their Lord and Savior and suffer eternal loss and ruin. The Spirit of Christ spoke through the Apostle Paul in *Romans 10:1* when he expressed that his ardent desire and prayer to God was that Israel might be saved.

Jesus still weeps over the lost condition of Israel today. But He has purchased their salvation for them through His death on the cross. All they have to do, like anyone else, is believe and receive Yeshua as their Messiah to be saved. We as a Church must in love, understanding, and patience give them that opportunity by sharing the Gospel with them. If we don't, they will remain lost without their true Messiah.

We must take the Gospel to the Jews of Jerusalem because God commands it. Preaching the Gospel to the Jews of Jerusalem, Israel, and the world is not an option for Bible-believing Christians. It is commanded by God in *Isaiah 40:9-10*. We are not only to bring the good tidings of salvation to Israel but we are to do it with boldness and strength.

Brethren, my heart's desire and prayer to God for Israel is that they may be saved.

Romans 10:1

F-R-I-E-N-D-S

An Acronym for Sharing the Love of Jesus with the Jewish People

Jewish people are like everybody else. They need to be introduced to the Savior Jesus and experience God's forgiveness from sin and have eternal life through Him. Two thousand years ago, Jesus, a born and bred Israeli Jew, came to this very people first to bring them such blessed realities. Indeed, our Lord stated this in *Matthew 15:24*: "***I was not sent except to the lost sheep of the house of Israel.***" The plain fact is that, like Gentiles, the Jews need the Gospel, particularly since the Messiah is Jewish and came to Israel for the express purpose of proclaiming the Gospel to them (*Mark 1:14-15; Luke 4:18*). This fact alone, if for no other, makes it imperative for Gentile believers in Jesus the Messiah to make known His saving grace to His own ethnic brothers and sisters.

In my varied gospel outreach experiences to the Jewish people, I have developed the acronym FRIENDS to lay out basic principles easy to remember as a guideline for sharing Jesus the Messiah with your Jewish friend or neighbor.

F - Friendship

R - Reach

I - Israel

E - Explain

N - Neutralize

D - Destiny

S - Savior

Friendship

Before engaging in a thought-provoking discussion about why Jesus is the Messiah with your Jewish neighbor (which is a serious thing for anyone to consider), you must first establish a bond of trust and friendship with that person. Some people approach evangelism in general, and Jewish evangelism in particular, with a numbers game mentality that places a greater emphasis on quantity (how many can be saved) instead of the quality of one's Gospel witness (the quality of one's witness). But with the Jewish person, you must earn the right to share your faith with them by gaining their respect. This involves befriending him or her with genuine love for them and a concern for their spiritual welfare.

Establishing a friendship with anyone means to take a keen interest in him or her, like how they think, and the particular background he or she comes from. It also means taking time and energy to know and understand that person as a unique individual made in the image of God. Friendship is a gift from God and one of the most important expressions of His love for establishing healthy and lasting relationships. It is a valuable way of connecting yourself with other people in the world we live in.

Reach

The very nature of taking the Gospel to the world means we must seek people out to share the saving message of Jesus the Messiah with them. Jesus commanded the Church to "***Go into all the world***" and preach the Gospel (*Matthew 28: 19-20*). "All the world" most certainly includes where the Jewish people live, too. In fact, they are the first people group who should hear the Gospel (*Romans 1:16*).

To reach your Jewish neighbor, you must develop a sincere desire to understand and know the history, religion, and customs of the Jewish people. These are the ancient people who gave us the Bible and the Messiah, and it behooves us to keep that in the forefront of our minds as we share what is a very Jewish message — the Gospel of Jesus the Messiah. You cannot preach until you are willing to reach.

Take the initiative and learn what it is to be Jewish — think Jewish — so that you can effectively reach them for Jesus. Paul utilized the accommodation principle of evangelism too when he said in *1 Corinthians 9:20*, "***To the Jews I became as a Jew that I might win Jews.***"

Israel

There are two ways to strengthen your effectiveness and credibility with the Jews. Read and believe the Scriptures, written cover to cover by Jews, then familiarize yourself with their 4,000-year history as the nation of Israel. The regathering and rebirth of the Jewish nation of Israel in May 1948 is indisputably the single greatest fulfillment of Bible prophecy since the time of Christ. The Bible foretold that at the end of days (that period of time immediately before the return of Christ), God would regather the Jewish people from worldwide dispersion and bring them back to their ancient homeland (*Deuteronomy 30:1-3; Isaiah 11:11-12; Jeremiah 12:14-15; Ezekiel 20:33-42; 37*).

For over 1900 years, the Jewish people were scattered throughout the world. They suddenly became a nation again in one day on May 14, 1948, after the travail and horrors of the holocaust a few years earlier. *Isaiah 66:7-9* predicted this very thing. Knowing the history of Israel and the divine destiny God has for them goes a long way in having an effective Gospel witness to them.

On several occasions, when I have shown these very same prophetic Scriptures to Jewish people to whom I am witnessing, they are utterly amazed at how the Bible exactly foretold their history as it has come to pass thus far. It makes them realize that the Bible has a divine Author who has accurately predicted their history and that Christians who lovingly demonstrate this to them have a deep respect and interest for their past, present, and future.

Explain

Once you can reasonably understand their history through the scriptures, you are able to more easily explain how believing in Jesus as the Messiah is a natural step for the Jewish person to take. That is, explain to the Jewish person how the Messianic prophecies in his Bible have been fulfilled by Jesus showing beyond all doubt He is the Messiah of the Jews. Most Jews today have not heard of Messianic prophecy simply because the study of it largely fell out of Judaism (except for some Orthodox circles) several centuries ago. Also most secular Jews today do not study the Bible seriously. Like many Christians in the church today, most Jews do not know their own Bible.

Prophecies about the Messiah were given to the Jews so that they could recognize Him when He came. The prophecies that mark His identity come from the Bible alone — the Hebrew Scriptures. Detailed prophecies about the Messiah's pre-existence, deity, lineage, birth, ministry, sufferings, death, resurrection, and ascension are given and are so exactly fulfilled in the life of Jesus that no one else has fulfilled or could fulfill them. Mastering the major Messianic prophecies from the Jewish Scriptures is a must for anyone who wants to effectively witness to Jews. (See *Messianic Prophecies* on page 21)

Jewish people have and will come to faith through these prophecies as the Holy Spirit works in them to convince them of the truth that Jesus is in fact the Messiah.

Neutralize

When witnessing to Jews about Jesus, you must be prepared for objections given against Jesus for not believing He is the Messiah. The purpose here is to neutralize such objections with informed and truthful information. Show them how believing in Jesus as the Messiah is a naturally Jewish thing to do instead of a Non-Jewish thing, as they are wrongly taught and led to believe. For nearly two thousand years Jewish people have been thoroughly indoctrinated by their rabbies, religious traditions, and culture to not believe Jesus is the Messiah.

Over the long centuries, the Church has treated the Jews deplorably as the Crusades, Inquisition, and Holocaust graphically testify. This mistreatment by alleged 'Christians' has greatly harmed the cause of Christ. Jews are taught that followers of Christ committed these horrible atrocities against their people. Therefore, they assume that most Christians hate Jews. This has built up a natural wall of resistance whenever Jews are told about Christ.

Answering these objections with a clear understanding of Jewish history and Scripture will go a long way in clearing up any misunderstanding between true Christians who are Philo-Semitic (they love the Jewish people) as opposed to pseudo-Christians who are Anti-Semitic. True followers of the Jewish Jesus will love His people because He loves them and chose them through whom He would come to redeem the world. Jesus said, "***salvation is of the Jews***" (*John 4:22*).

Showing a sincere interest and knowledge of your Jewish friends' religion and history will no doubt impress them with the fact that you took enough time to study and understand their culture. I remember sharing with a group of young Israelis at a Kibbutz about certain key events in Jewish history. One of the individuals was so impressed by this that she remarked, "You know our history better than I do." This provided a golden opportunity to share the Gospel with the group.

Destiny

We must learn and know the divine destiny of the Chosen People as central to the Messiah so that we can make them see that the Gospel message directly pertains to them. God has chosen the Jewish people to fulfill a divine destiny. An

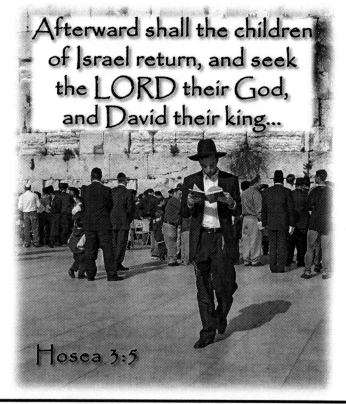

Afterward shall the children of Israel return, and seek the LORD their God, and David their king...

Hosea 3:5

integral part of that destiny involves, of course, knowing and recognizing Jesus as the Jewish Messiah. God chose the Jews to receive and write the Holy Scriptures (*Exodus 24:4-8; Romans 3:2*), to reveal the character of the one true God to the nations of the world (Isaiah 43:10), and to bring the promised Redeemer (*Genesis 22:18; Galatians 3:15-16*). The Jews' future destiny will involve the complete restoration of their nation (which is partially taking place now) returning them to their ancient homeland of Israel for national salvation when Messiah Jesus returns to Israel with power and great glory (*Zechariah 12:10; Romans 11:26-27*).

Israel's hope is not in their military prowess, or in America's ongoing support for their survival, but in the Savior Who alone can save them.

The problems for the Jew and the Gentile that stand between him and God are sin. Sin separates us from God. God's Word tells us the only way this barrier can be bridged between the sinner and God is that appropriate blood atonement must be made (*Leviticus 17:11*). The animal sacrifices of the Old Testament provided only a temporary covering for these sins and pointed to the once-and-for-all final sacrifice of Messiah Jesus, granting full and final pardon to the Jew and Gentile who believe. God's final and perfect blood atonement came by way of Messiah Jesus (*Isaiah 53; Hebrews 9-10*). This free gift of the Messiah is received by faith through the prayer of a believing heart.

We at B'rit Hadashah have and will always endeavor to implement the FRIENDS acronym in our Gospel witness to Jews in Israel. It works. Do the same and watch God move in your witness and bring Jewish souls to Jesus the Messiah.

And beginning at Moses and all the Prophets, He expounded to them in all the Scriptures the things concerning Himself.

Luke 24:27

CHAPTER 3:
Messianic Prophecies

On the following pages, you will find a list of the major Messianic prophecies found in the Old Testament that were fulfilled in the New Testament in the life of Jesus of Nazareth. This list is one to which we commonly and often appeal when arguing the case for Jesus being the Jewish Messiah with the Jewish people to whom we witness in Israel.

Although Jesus fulfilled over three hundred prophecies made about the Messiah in the Old Testament, this list is a compilation of the more familair ones that give a complete portrait of the One foretold to come by Moses and all the prophets from Genesis to Malachi. Knowing where these prophecies are in the Old Testament and how Jesus fulfilled them in the New Testament is fundamental to effective Jewish evangelism and critical for making the case to the Jewish person that Jesus is in fact the one true Messiah of Israel. Any serious-minded Christian who wants to share his faith with the Chosen People should know and master this basic list.

OLD TESTAMENT PROPHECY

To be born in Bethlehem...

Micah 5:2
"But you, Bethlehem Ephrathah, Though you are little among the thousands of Judah, Yet out of you shall come forth to Me The One to be Ruler in Israel, Whose goings forth are from of old, From everlasting."

The Son of God...

Psalm 2:7
"I will declare the decree: The LORD has said to Me, 'You are My Son, Today I have begotten You.'"

Of the tribe of Judah...

Genesis 49:10
"The scepter shall not depart from Judah, Nor a lawgiver from between his feet, Until Shiloh comes; And to Him shall be the obedience of the people."

Of a virgin...

Isaiah 7:14
"Therefore the Lord Himself will give you a sign: Behold, the virgin shall conceive and bear a Son, and shall call His name Immanuel."

NEW TESTAMENT FULFILLMENT

Matthew 2:1-5

"Now after Jesus was born in Bethlehem of Judea in the days of Herod the king, behold, wise men from the East came to Jerusalem, saying, "Where is He who has been born King of the Jews? For we have seen His star in the East and have come to worship Him." When Herod the king heard this, he was troubled, and all Jerusalem with him. And when he had gathered all the chief priests and scribes of the people together, he inquired of them where the Christ was to be born. So they said to him, "In Bethlehem of Judea, for thus it is written by the prophet...'"

John 3:16-17

"For God so loved the world that He gave His only begotten Son, that whoever believes in Him should not perish but have everlasting life. For God did not send His Son into the world to condemn the world, but that the world through Him might be saved."

Hebrews 7:14

"For it is evident that our Lord arose from Judah, of which tribe Moses spoke nothing concerning priesthood."

Matthew 1:18-21

"Now the birth of Jesus Christ was as follows: After His mother Mary was betrothed to Joseph, before they came together, she was found with child of the Holy Spirit. Then Joseph her husband, being a just man, and not wanting to make her a public example, was minded to put her away secretly. But while he thought about these things, behold, an angel of the Lord appeared to him in a dream, saying, 'Joseph, son of David, do not be afraid to take to you Mary your wife, for that which is conceived in her is of the Holy Spirit. And she will bring forth a Son, and you shall call His name JESUS, for He will save His people from their sins.'"

OLD TESTAMENT PROPHECY

A prophet like Moses...
Deuteronomy 18:15
" 'The LORD your God will raise up for you a Prophet like me from your midst, from your brethren. Him you shall hear,..."

The King of Israel...
Zechariah 9:9
"Rejoice greatly, O daughter of Zion! Shout, O daughter of Jerusalem! Behold, your King is coming to you; He is just and having salvation, Lowly and riding on a donkey, A colt, the foal of a donkey."

Rejected...
Isaiah 53:3
"He is despised and rejected by men, A Man of sorrows and acquainted with grief. And we hid, as it were, our faces from Him; He was despised, and we did not esteem Him."

Beaten...
Micah 5:1
"Now gather yourself in troops, O daughter of troops; He has laid siege against us; They will strike the judge of Israel with a rod on the cheek."

Silent...
Isaiah 53:7
"He was oppressed and He was afflicted, Yet He opened not His mouth; He was led as a lamb to the laughter, And as a sheep before its shearers is silent, So He opened not His mouth."

NEW TESTAMENT FULFILLMENT

John 7:15-17

"And the Jews marveled, saying, "How does this Man know letters, having never studied?" Jesus answered them and said, "My doctrine is not Mine, but His who sent Me. If anyone wills to do His will, he shall know concerning the doctrine, whether it is from God or whether I speak on My own authority."

John 12:12-15

"The next day a great multitude that had come to the feast, when they heard that Jesus was coming to Jerusalem, took branches of palm trees and went out to meet Him, and cried out: 'Hosanna! Blessed is He who comes in the name of the LORD! The King of Israel!' Then Jesus, when He had found a young donkey, sat on it; as it is written: 'Fear not, daughter of Zion; Behold, your King is coming, Sitting on a donkey's colt.'"

John 1:11

"He came to His own, and His own did not receive Him."

Mark 15:19

Then they struck Him on the head with a reed and spat on Him; and bowing the knee, they worshiped Him.

Matthew 27:12-14

"And while He was being accused by the chief priests and elders, He answered nothing. Then Pilate said to Him, 'Do You not hear how many things they testify against You?' But He answered him not one word, so that the governor marveled greatly."

OLD TESTAMENT PROPHECY

Betrayed...

Psalm 41:9

"*Even my own familiar friend in whom I trusted, Who ate my bread, Has lifted up his heel against me.*"

Tried and condemned...

Isaiah 53:8

"*He was taken from prison and from judgment, And who will declare His generation? For He was cut off from the land of the living; For the transgressions of My people He was stricken.*"

Crucified...

Psalm 22:16

"*For dogs have surrounded Me; The congregation of the wicked has enclosed Me. They pierced My hands and My feet;*"

His garments divided...

Psalm 22:18

"*They divide My garments among them, And for My clothing they cast lots.*"

Given vinegar and gall...

Psalm 69:21

"*They also gave me gall for my food, And for my thirst they gave me vinegar to drink.*"

NEW TESTAMENT FULFILLMENT

Mark 14:17-20

"In the evening He came with the twelve. Now as they sat and ate, Jesus said, 'Assuredly, I say to you, one of you who eats with Me will betray Me.' And they began to be sorrowful, and to say to Him one by one, 'Is it I?' And another said, 'Is it I?' He answered and said to them, 'It is one of the twelve, who dips with Me in the dish.'"

Matthew 27:1-2

"When morning came, all the chief priests and elders of the people plotted against Jesus to put Him to death. And when they had bound Him, they led Him away and delivered Him to Pontius Pilate the governor."

John 19:17-18

"And He, bearing His cross, went out to a place called the Place of a Skull, which is called in Hebrew, Golgotha, where they crucified Him, and two others with Him, one on either side, and Jesus in the center."

John 19:23-24

"Then the soldiers, when they had crucified Jesus, took His garments and made four parts, to each soldier a part, and also the tunic. Now the tunic was without seam, woven from the top in one piece. They said therefore among themselves, 'Let us not tear it, but cast lots for it, whose it shall be,' that the Scripture might be fulfilled which says: 'They divided My garments among them, And for My clothing they cast lots.' Therefore the soldiers did these things."

John 19:28-29

"After this, Jesus, knowing that all things were now accomplished, that the Scripture might be fulfilled, said, 'I thirst!' Now a vessel full of sour wine was sitting there; and they filled a sponge with sour wine, put it on hyssop, and put it to His mouth."

OLD TESTAMENT PROPHECY

His bones not broken...

Exodus 12:46

"In one house it shall be eaten; you shall not carry any of the flesh outside the house, nor shall you break one of its bones."

He is our sacrifice...

Isaiah 53:5-6

"But He was wounded for our transgressions, He was bruised for our iniquities; The chastisement for our peace was upon Him, And by His stripes we are healed. All we like sheep have gone astray; We have turned, every one, to his own way; And the LORD has laid on Him the iniquity of us all."

And raised from death!

Psalm 16:10

"For You will not leave my soul in Sheol, Nor will You allow Your Holy One to see corruption."

NEW TESTAMENT FULFILLMENT

John 19:31-36

"Therefore, because it was the Preparation Day, that the bodies should not remain on the cross on the Sabbath (for that Sabbath was a high day), the Jews asked Pilate that their legs might be broken, and that they might be taken away. Then the soldiers came and broke the legs of the first and of the other who was crucified with Him. But when they came to Jesus and saw that He was already dead, they did not break His legs. But one of the soldiers pierced His side with a spear, and immediately blood and water came out. And he who has seen has testified, and his testimony is true; and he knows that he is telling the truth, so that you may believe. For these things were done that the Scripture should be fulfilled, 'Not one of His bones shall be broken.'"

I Peter 2:24-25

"who Himself bore our sins in His own body on the tree, that we, having died to sins, might live for righteousness—by whose stripes you were healed. For you were like sheep going astray, but have now returned to the Shepherd and Overseer of your souls."

Luke 24:1-7,47

"Now on the first day of the week, very early in the morning, they, and certain other women with them, came to the tomb bringing the spices which they had prepared. But they found the stone rolled away from the tomb. Then they went in and did not find the body of the Lord Jesus. And it happened, as they were greatly perplexed about this, that behold, two men stood by them in shining garments. Then, as they were afraid and bowed their faces to the earth, they said to them, 'Why do you seek the living among the dead? He is not here, but is risen! Remember how He spoke to you when He was still in Galilee, saying, "The Son of Man must be delivered into the hands of sinful men, and be crucified, and the third day rise again."'"

¹¹It shall come to pass in that day
That the Lord shall set His hand again the
second time
To recover the remnant of His people who
are left,
From Assyria and Egypt,
From Pathros and Cush,
From Elam and Shinar,
From Hamath and the islands of the sea.
¹²He will set up a banner for the nations,
And will assemble the outcasts of Israel,
And gather together the dispersed of Judah
From the four corners of the earth.

Isaiah 11:11-12

CHAPTER 4:
The Early Encounters

March 2001 - *Todd was joined by Kevin Parker, an Israel tour leader for Zola Levitt Ministries. This was their first evangelistic mission to Israel.*

While in Jerusalem, we went to Mt. Zion where the tomb of David and the Upper Room are closely situated. There is a small synagogue in the room with David's tomb. There, on the Sabbath day, Kevin and I were led to talk with two Yeshiva (Jewish seminary) students, studying to be rabbis, about how Yeshua of Nazareth fulfilled many of the Messianic prophecies, with special emphasis on the Messianic Psalms. By the way, one of the young men, named Menachem, was reading the Psalms from the Hebrew text before we came into the room!

We shared with them from the Hebrew text about prophecies that foretold the Messiah's virgin birth (*Gen. 3:15; Is. 7:14*); where He would be born (*Mic. 5:2*); the manner of His death (*Ps. 22*); His resurrection from the dead (*Ps. 16:10-11*) and His glorious return, when the Jews are regathered to Israel from dispersion and Jerusalem is excavated from ruins and rebuilt (*Hos. 3:3-5; Ps. 102:12-16*). We spent almost an hour with them. They were intrigued and said they would give this important matter serious attention and study.

Please pray that the Holy Spirit will open their eyes and hearts to accept Yeshua as Lord and Messiah.

Tomb of David

A young Orthodox Jew studies at the Western Wall

✝ ✡ ✝ ✡ ✝ ✡ ✝

Another incident in Jerusalem involved an intense debate between three Sephardic (Middle-Eastern Jewish) students of a Torah school. Later, we found out that our discussion with them had taken place just outside four synagogues joined together. The hour-long debate centered on who Yeshua was, and how only by a blood sacrifice can the sinner be cleansed and forgiven in the sight of God (*Lev. 17:11*). When they admitted that keeping the Law and following rabbinical tradition was not sufficient enough for salvation, and that only an acceptable blood sacrifice could save, they acknowledged their nation was in trouble, having no Temple, priests, or sacrifice for nearly two thousand years!

Then we preached to them about the reality of the New Covenant, which has already been ratified with the house of Israel through the once-for-all perfect sacrifice of the Messiah (*Jer. 31:31–34; Matt. 26:27–28*). Sadly, they rejected this saving truth, stumbling over the simplicity of it and taking offense at a crucified Messiah (*1 Cor. 1:23; 1 Pet. 2:8*).

✝ ✡ ✝ ✡ ✝ ✡ ✝

In Galilee, the Lord gave us several witnessing opportunities. The people there were generally receptive, grateful, and some very moved as we told them how God is bound to the Jewish people through the eternal, immutable and unconditional covenants (namely, the Abrahamic, Davidic, and New Covenants).

One evening, Kevin and I noticed an elderly woman with a walking cane badly limping along in pain. We went back down the stairs and greeted her. Her name was Naomi and she had multiple sclerosis. Kevin gave his personal testimony about the intense struggle he and his wife Leighanne went through during her time of illness. Through it all, he told Naomi, God sustained and strengthened them, transforming a tragedy into a triumph.

We told her the only way that could have happened is the fact that Yeshua the Messiah came and took our infirmities and bore our sicknesses (*Is. 53:4; Matt 8:17*). We further told her that He defeated death by His resurrection and that He personally wanted to carry the heavy load of her crippling disease upon His shoulders (*Matt 11:28–30*). She was moved to tears. We ended up giving her a Messianic Jewish Gospel tract and a Hebrew New Testament, with assurances of keeping her in our prayers.

A breathtaking view of the Sea of Galilee

✝ ✡ ✝ ✡ ✝ ✡ ✝

The Lord saved His best for last. While on the plane coming back to the States, the Lord gave us the opportunity to share with a Russian Jewish lady from New York City. Her name was Nadia. She had stayed in Jerusalem for three weeks visiting her relatives on her first trip to the Holy Land. We shared with her how God sent us over there to comfort and encourage the Jewish people with the good news of Yeshua the Messiah.

Surprisingly, she responded by telling us that an Israeli tour guide who was a Messianic Jew said the same things to her in Jerusalem. We went over the Gospel with her via a Messianic Jewish tract. After she carefully read it we asked if she would like to receive Yeshua the Jewish Messiah in her heart. **She gladly prayed with us and was born again on the spot!**

After she did this she exclaimed with visible relief and joy on her face, "Now I feel such a peace." Yes, that is because the Prince of Peace lives in Nadia now. We cannot thank the Lord, Zola, and the Shalom, Shalom congregation enough for allowing us the inestimable privilege of sharing the Gospel of Yeshua the Messiah with His Chosen People.

September 2001 - Again, Todd was joined by Kevin Parker

On this evangelistic outreach to the Jewish people of Israel, Kevin Parker and I learned the seed faith principle of witnessing. That is to say that we sowed much gospel seed in Israel knowing by faith that the harvest of those we touched would eventually come in the Lord's appointed season. We cannot reap Jewish souls for the Messiah Jesus until we first plant that seed and wait for its growth. Patience and persistence has been given to us by God and is needed when preaching the Gospel to the Chosen People. With this understanding, our sowing of the Gospel began the very day we arrived at our hotel in Jerusalem. As we were checking in, we got into a discussion with two of the desk clerks about God's plan for Israel and the Messiah's soon return.

Kevin and I briefly shared how the birth of the modern nation of Israel on May 14, 1948, was a fulfillment of Bible prophecy in *Isaiah 66:7–9* — an amazing prophecy that we often referred to in our witnessing on this trip. After we presented the historic and prophetic overview of God's plan for Israel from Scripture, one of them, struck with amazement, replied, "That is heavy." We left them with Gospel tracts detailing what we had shared. Throughout our stay at the Dan Pearl Hotel in Jerusalem, God gave us the opportunity to share the Gospel about Yeshua the Jewish Messiah with staff and guests staying there. They were open, appreciative, and received the Gospel tracts and Hebrew New Testaments we gave out.

✝ ✿ ✝ ✿ ✝ ✿ ✝

On this trip we tried a new witnessing method on Jaffa Street that put us in a passive role, allowing the Holy Spirit to take the lead (as He always should in every evangelistic activity) in literally bringing Jewish people to us. After prayer one morning, prompted by the Holy Spirit, Kevin suggested we go and sit on a sidewalk bench along the street where

Israeli pedestrians pass. When we arrived, we laid out our Gospel literature and Hebrew New Testaments. Several Jewish people came up to see what we had laid out and this afforded us several opportunities to share the Messiah with them. Before our very eyes, God was drawing those He pre-ordained to hear and ultimately believe (see *John 6:44*). While we were witnessing to an American-born Jew and an Ethiopian Jew, two young Orthodox Jewish adolescents who were from an anti-missionary group suddenly came riding up on bicycles to disrupt our conversation.

They began yelling in Hebrew and strictly charged the two men not to listen to us. We told them that Israel was a democracy and that we have the freedom and right to express our views there. Then to our amazement, Kevin and I stood back and watched how the Spirit of God waged and won this battle for us. Instead of yelling back at the anti-missionaries ourselves, the two we were sharing the Gospel with came to our defense and we simply watched as they brushed them aside. Yes, our God does fight for us (*Nehemiah 4:20*). The anti-missionaries were frustrated and finally left while the other two remained behind to hear the rest of our message, receiving Gospel tracts and Hebrew New Testaments.

✢ ✿ ✢ ✿ ✢ ✿ ✢

On Mount Zion, we came across an Orthodox Jewish organization called The World Center for Peace. The group offers a free twenty-minute presentation on why Jesus is not the Messiah. Kevin and I felt led by the Holy Spirit to challenge and provide sound rebuttal from Scripture on why Jesus is the Messiah. We entered the place and listened to the twenty-minute presentation by an Orthodox Jew named Eliyahu. The sum of his argument, which was quite weak and unconvincing, was that Jesus could not have been the Messiah since He did not overthrow Israel's enemies and establish a successful rule. We counter-argued that the Messiah came the first time to suffer and die for the sins of Israel and the world in order to bring redemption and reconciliation to all who accept Him. Our texts were *Isaiah 53* and *Psalm 22.* We said further that when He comes again, the Messiah will rescue Israel and establish His universal rule at that time (*Zech. 12, 14; Psalm 2*). The man could not answer the fact that the specific prophetic details about the suffering, death, burial and resurrection of the Servant of the Lord made in Isaiah 53 fit exactly with the manner in which Jesus suffered, died, was buried and then raised. He further had to admit when pressed from Scripture that the Messiah should have come before the second temple was destroyed (see *Malachi 3:1; Haggai 2:9; Daniel 9:25–26*), which Jesus as the Messiah did.

We argued our case well for Jesus as Messiah, and for every objection he gave, Kevin and I gave him ten reasons why Jesus was, in fact, the long expected One. By doing this, we simply followed the apostolic pattern by debating with the Jews to prove Jesus is the Messiah from their own Scriptures (see *Acts 9:22; 17:2–3; 18:5*). After an hour and a half debate, we left having planted a seed of doubt in his mind about his position. We pray that seed will yield faith in Jesus as the only true Messiah of Israel.

Todd shares with Israelis in the Jewish Quarter of the Old City

✝ ✡ ✝ ✡ ✝ ✡ ✝

During the latter part of our stay in Jerusalem, we decided one evening to go back to a restaurant called The Rosemary

Café to follow up on a young lady we had shared the Gospel with in April. She no longer worked there. But the Lord gave us an excellent opportunity to share the Gospel with a new waitress — a young girl named Miach. We discussed with her about the special and divine destiny God has for the Jewish people revealed both in the Tanach (Old Testament) and B'rit Hadashah (New Testament), both books written by Jews from cover to cover. She listened with great interest. We explained that God created her to have a personal relationship with Him through the Messiah Jesus, which is experienced through faith. The fact is that Yeshua came as the Messiah to die for our sins on the tree so that we could have forgiveness. He then rose from death to give us eternal life and a home in heaven with His heavenly Father.

She responded by telling us that she was unsatisfied and empty going to the synagogue. She was visibly touched by what we said and told us, "You are both special." In reply, we told her that her people were truly special because God chose them to record His revelation to man and to redeem the world through the Jewish Messiah Jesus — the Jew of all Jews (*John 4:22; Romans 3:2; 9:3–5; 15:8*). As we left, she said she would read the Gospel tract and Hebrew New Testament and seriously think about accepting Jesus in her life.

✝ ✿ ✝ ✿ ✝ ✿ ✝

The providential timing of God and the sovereign way the Holy Spirit led us as we witnessed throughout Israel was powerfully evident every day. One example of an event in Galilee illustrates this. Kevin and I decided to walk among the shops in Tiberias. As we walked for some time in that area, there seemed to be no opportunities open for us to witness to the Jewish people. Frustrated over this seeming impasse, I began to silently pray that unbelieving Israel would come to faith in Jesus as the Jewish Messiah and that someone in that area would be open to our testimony.

The Holy Spirit then led me to claim the promise of *Joshua 1:3* so that the Gospel we proclaim would have a ruling influence in that place wherever the soles of our feet walked. The verse in Joshua in its historical context was given to Joshua and Israel as they were about to go into the hostile territory of Canaan to claim ownership over the land God promised them. Little did we know how quickly this would play out in a spiritual manner.

Shortly after this silent prayer, Kevin and I stopped at a restaurant called Cherry's. When our waitress came to our table to take our order, we started talking to her about the World Trade Center bombing. This tragic event, more than anything else, was a constant door opener to witness and share the Gospel with Israel. At some point in the conversation, we discussed the soon return of the Messiah and she became hostile and flat out said she did not believe in Him. She then left momentarily.

A mother and daughter sitting at the next table overheard our conversation. She expressed her appreciation about what we said. She was an Orthodox Jew. We talked to her about the restoration and central role Israel will play during end-time Bible prophecy that is a major sign of Messiah's return. We attempted to give her a Messianic Jewish tract showing Jesus is the Messiah. She declined, at first, and said that they had to leave to catch the bus. But about a minute later, she surprised us by coming back into the restaurant and said she would in fact take and read the tract we offered.

The waitress saw this and took offense. She came back to our table and said in a tone of obvious hostility, "Is there a problem here?" Instead of taking offense, we replied softly and tenderly what we had just told the lady and her daughter about God's plan for Israel as revealed in Scripture and how it shows Jesus is the Messiah of Israel. To our great marvel, her hostile demeanor toward the Gospel began changing to an openness and willingness to listen. The Holy Spirit through our witness and testimony was transforming her attitude right before our eyes! Such a change was especially indicated by the fact that we asked if she wanted a free copy of a Hebrew New Testament. The first time she outright refused. Later on, when we asked her again, she said she would think about it. After we finished our meal, we asked a third time. She not only took it but also took a Gospel tract and thanked us for them! May God continue the change in her heart and produce the new birth by faith in the Jewish Messiah as she reads the B'rit Hadashah and receives the words of Jesus in the original language He spoke them in.

✝ ✧ ✝ ✧ ✝ ✧ ✝

A few days later, Kevin and I were in the Yardenit Gift Shop. Led by the Spirit, we initiated a conversation with two young Jewish ladies — one was named Hagar. They were eagerly open to our witness and teaching about Jesus, the Gospel, and the divine role of Israel in history. They were simply amazed about what the God of Israel has done, is doing, and will do for the Chosen People. They were thrilled about us giving them free Hebrew New Testaments. As we left the gift shop, another young lady, one of Hagar's friends, came up and wanted a Hebrew New Testament, too. They invited us to eat with them and other friends in the cafeteria. All together there were six young Israeli girls who joined us for lunch who were all working on the Kinneret Kibbutz.

Kevin and I spent over an hour with the group discussing the existence of God and Jesus being the true Messiah of Israel. They asked why we believed this about Jesus. Our clear answer was because He fulfilled all the prophecies made in the Tanach (Old Testament) that foretold events of His first coming centuries before He was born. Four of the girls were secular and two were nominally religious.

When the hour had past and our conversation concluded with them, one of the secular girls exclaimed, "You have opened my eyes!" No doubt God's Spirit is at work again in Israel. The veil and partial blindness of unbelief over Israelis toward their Messiah Jesus is beginning to lift as the coming of the Lord draws very near and the fullness of the Gentiles during the Church age is quickly coming to a close *(see Romans 11:25–26; 2 Corinthians 3:13–16).*

One of the original olive trees in the Garden of Gethsemane that stood during Jesus' time

¹² But You, O LORD, shall endure forever,
And the remembrance of Your name to all
generations.
¹³ You will arise and have mercy on Zion;
For the time to favor her,
Yes, the set time, has come.
¹⁴ For Your servants take pleasure in her stones,
And show favor to her dust.
¹⁵ So the nations shall fear the name of the
LORD,
And all the kings of the earth Your glory.
¹⁶ For the LORD shall build up Zion;
He shall appear in His glory.

Psalm 102:12-16

CHAPTER 5:

Partners in His Commission

March 2002 - *Todd was joined by Kevin Parker a third time*

O nce again Zola Levitt Ministries and Shalom, Shalom Messianic Congregation partnered and commissioned Kevin Parker and me to Israel to bring the hope, peace, and love of Yeshua the Messiah to the Chosen People. This was our third consecutive Gospel outreach to them.

Our encounters with the Israelis found them particularly open and receptive to our message of support and love based on the Scriptures. God's divine plan and program for the Jewish people, finds completion in both the first and second comings of the Messiah.

In the wake of terrorist attacks and international censure by the media and pro-Palestinian governments, the Israelis we met eagerly listened to the message of redemption, victory, and restoration for Israel. In a time when most Jews in Israel feel hopeless, misunderstood, abandoned by the world, and betrayed in some measure by America's incoherent and duplicitous Mid-East policy, God's Spirit worked through us to reassure them they are not alone. Here are a few of the many experiences we had in taking the Jewish Gospel to the Jewish people.

✝ ✿ ✝ ✿ ✝ ✿ ✝

In Tel Aviv, we walked the streets and visited the cafes (one of which was bombed a few days later by a suicide bomber). We stopped in the shops, encouraging the Jewish people from the Scriptures that God has not forsaken them (*Isaiah 49:14–16*). One Jewish man we spoke with was the owner of an internet cafe. In our witness to him, we plunged into a deep discussion of what Bible prophecy says about the Messiah and His relationship to Israel. We covered topics such as the regathering of Israel, the future war of Gog and Magog as predicted in *Ezekiel 38–39*, and the return of the Messiah. He was open and interested in the evidence from the Tanach (Old Testament) that proved Yeshua (Jesus) was the prophesied Messiah. The Holy Spirit no doubt had prepared this man's heart for our preaching. He gratefully received, and even enthusiastically anticipated, our giving him a Hebrew New Testament (B'rit Hadashah) and a Messianic Jewish tract that lays out the steps to salvation. As we were leaving, the man's parting yet memorable remark to us was: "Thank you for bringing me the light." How correct he was! Jesus said in *John 9:5, "I am the light of the world."*

✝ ✡ ✝ ✡ ✝ ✡ ✝

After four days in Tel Aviv, we drove to the Galilee to begin our outreach there. One day while we witnessed and passed out Gospel tracts, three Jewish children came over to us and wanted to play. Little did Kevin and I realize that these seven-year-old children (triplets — two boys and one girl) would be instrumental in opening the door for us to minister the Gospel to their entire family for three days. *"And a child shall lead them" (Isaiah 11:6)*. We became close to the family almost immediately, so much so that they invited us to stay with them when we returned in September.

We spent the entire time discussing the divine calling and plan of God for Israel as revealed in the Bible and how this fits with the current crisis in Israel (*see Deut 4:28–30; Ezek.*

The Keres family at home in Tel Aviv

35; Ps. 83; Zech. 12–14). They read with amazement from the Scriptures how all this was foretold long ago, and how it is being fulfilled up to the present time.

We reasoned with them that if the prophecies of Israel's history are true and have literally been fulfilled, then the many prophecies about the Messiah were also true and have been literally fulfilled as well. This was the warp and woof of our witness in all of Israel. We pointed to the prophecies that pertain to the first coming of the Messiah in the Tanach, and then pointed to their exact fulfillment by Jesus in the B'rit Hadashah. These dear friends made the obvious connection and understood quite clearly from their own Scriptures why we believe Jesus is the Jewish Messiah.

Through our witness of the Gospel both in love and in the spoken word, this family has adopted Kevin and me as lifelong friends. We believe it is only a matter of time before they become a household of believers in Yeshua (*Acts 16:31, 34*).

✝ ✡ ✝ ✡ ✝ ✡ ✝

A few days later, we ventured into Tiberias during the evening and decided to eat at one of the restaurants, eventually striking up a conversation with the owner's son. He was a Jewish man of twenty-three years and had lived in New York City. He told us he worked a block and a half away from the World Trade Center and was a personal eyewitness of what happened on 9-11. He was still suffering from post-traumatic stress. He knew he had to return home — to Israel.

He revealed to us later that he had also been taking narcotics and felt tormented and controlled by an evil spirit! We explained to him that there was a battle going on for his soul between God and Satan, and that only the power of Messiah could set him free. Kevin and I then demonstrated to him out of the Jewish Scriptures from the Hebrew text that Jesus was indeed the prophesied Messiah of Israel who came to set humanity free from the captivity of sin (*John 8:34–36*). After looking at a few of the prophecies for himself, he exclaimed, "Yeshua really is the Messiah!"

The young man became teary-eyed and prayed with us to accept Yeshua into his heart as Lord, Savior and Messiah. Afterwards, his face glowed with the peace, joy and relief that only the Prince of Peace can give. He is now a new creation, a completed Jew born anew and delivered from the power of darkness, translated into the kingdom of God's beloved Son (*Colossians 1:13*). What a thrill it is to harvest souls for our Lord!

✝ ✡ ✝ ✡ ✝ ✡ ✝

From Tiberias, we journeyed to Jerusalem to conclude our ministry there. While staying at Kibbutz Tzuba, the Lord allowed us to minister restoration to a backslidden Jewish believer who had been a pioneer of the Messianic movement in the 1970s. At first he was guarded and distant. But after two days with him, the walls came down. He too was on the verge of tears as we extended God's grace and comfort to him and helped to relieve him from the heavy burden that was on his shoulders (*Galatians 6:1–2*).

The modern day village of Cana where Jesus changed the water into wine

✝ ✡ ✝ ✡ ✝ ✡ ✝

On Good Friday, as Kevin and I were coming from Golgotha (the place where Jesus was crucified), we ran into three young orthodox Jewish men in the Armenian quarter as they were headed for prayer at the Western Wall. Our witness to them naturally focused on why Jesus is the

Messiah of Israel. We talked about what the rabbis called in Hebrew the "Chevlei Ha Mashiach" (the birth pangs of the Messiah) as the time of the Great Tribulation for Israel, accompanied by certain cosmic signs (apostasy, false Messiahs, wars, earthquakes, famines, pestilences, etc.). These signs serve as guideposts for the soon return of the Messiah *(see Matthew 24)*. We told them that what Israel and Jerusalem are going through now is a prelude to those future events that indicate the fact that the Messiah is coming soon (*Zech. 14:1–3; Jer. 25:15–38; Ps. 83; Joel 3:1–2*).

Golgotha, the Place of the Skull, where Jesus was crucified

They listened as Kevin and I recited the major Messianic prophecies that mark and identify who the Messiah would be when He came and how the life of Jesus of Nazareth was the only One who could have possibly fulfilled these prophecies. They expressed sincere interest and took Gospel tracts from us and said they would study further what we shared with them.

Truly this Gospel outreach and others like it in the Church are fulfilling the prophecy of *Isaiah 62:10–12*! Here we have an amazing prophecy that says God will send Gentile believers to Jerusalem "*from the ends of the earth*" to proclaim to the Jewish inhabitants of Jerusalem that the Savior is coming to redeem and rescue them. These ambassadors of Messiah Jesus will prepare the way for His soon return that is described and predicted in the opening chapter of *Isaiah 63*.

[26] *And so all Israel will be saved, as it is written:*
" The Deliverer will come out of Zion,
And He will turn away ungodliness from Jacob;
[27] *For this is My covenant with them,*
When I take away their sins. "

Romans 11:26-27

CHAPTER 6:

Miracle

of

Replenishment

September 2002 - *Todd's fourth mission trip to Israel, this time accompanied by John Gonzales*

Our fourth Gospel outreach to the Jewish people of Israel covered a two-week period from September 14 to September 28, during the feasts of Yom Kippur and Tabernacles. John Gonzalez and I witnessed throughout the cities of Tel Aviv, Galilee, Qiryat Shimona and Jerusalem.

By the power of God's grace, our Gospel witness literally began the moment we landed on the tarmac at Ben Gurion Airport and continued right up to our last day in Israel. At passport control we were stopped and questioned about the purpose of our trip. We simply told them that we came to tell the Jewish people that Yeshua the Messiah has come to bring peace, fulfillment and forgiveness to the individual hearts of Jewish men and women. We said that Zola Levitt Ministries and Shalom Shalom Messianic Congregation sent us to comfort, encourage and pray for them during the intifada. One of the ladies from passport control wanted some proof of our ministry in Dallas, Texas. We pulled out a Zola Levitt Messianic prophecy bookmark that listed the major prophecies of the Messiah in the Tanach (Old Testament) and their corresponding fulfillment by Yeshua of Nazareth in the B'rit Hadashah (New Testament).

The three Israeli security women gathered around to look at these prophecies, intrigued and fascinated with these prophetic truths. One of them commented, "I have never heard of this before." How ironic. The Bible, the Messiah and the Gospel message all came from the Jewish people, and yet many Israelis today are in the dark about these most important things; all the more reason why they must hear the good news of Jesus the Messiah.

☦ ✿ ☦ ✿ ☦ ✿ ☦

While in Tel Aviv, we were walking in a public park and struck up a conversation with a young Jewish man who was walking to his motorcycle. Our discussion focused on Israel — the land of divine destiny — and how God has brought the Jewish people back to the Promised Land as a major fulfillment of Bible prophecy.

Like many secular Israelis, this man believed that giving the Palestinians more land could solve the Arab-Israeli conflict and that people should not dispute ownership of the land anyway since all land is the same. In reply, we suggested to him that the God of Israel set apart the Promised Land and Jerusalem to reveal His character and plan for the ages, namely, the Gospel of the Messiah through the Jewish people to the world *(see 1 Chronicles 16:14–24; 2 Chronicles 6:6; Ezekiel 5:5)*.

His philosophy was a mixture of monism and pantheism — the belief that all is one and that one is God. He also expressed the pluralistic idea that there were many good messianic figures, wise men and gurus down through history. But we pointed out that what makes Yeshua of Nazareth stand apart as the one true Messiah of Israel and the world, in contrast to these Messianic pretenders, is the indisputable fact that God raised Him from the dead. His tomb remains empty in Jerusalem as historic proof of this. No other guru or religious leader has done this. The man listened with interest and received a Gospel tract explaining the Gospel of Jesus and the divine plan for Israel throughout history.

A picture of the Garden Tomb where Jesus Christ rose from the dead

✝ ✡ ✝ ✡ ✝ ✡ ✝

On the eve of Yom Kippur (The Day of Atonement), we stopped in the Sheraton Hotel to have coffee. As we were looking for an entrance, a security guard appeared and told us that the restaurant was closed. We then told him that we were sent by a Messianic congregation in Dallas, Texas, to let the Jewish people know that God's plan for them is right on schedule and irrevocable (*Romans 11:29*). God chose Israel to bless all the nations of the earth, which He has certainly done with the Jewish Scriptures and the Jewish Messiah bringing salvation to those who believe (*Genesis 12:1–3; Romans 3:2; 9:5*). He smiled appreciatively at this support.

We talked to him about the evidence from the Jewish Scriptures that proves Yeshua is the Messiah of Israel and that the miraculous restoration of the Jewish people back to their ancient homeland is both a fulfillment of Bible prophecy and a sure sign of the Messiah's return. We showed him the prophecy of *Jeremiah 12:15–16* in Hebrew and English, which predicts that the Lord will remove the enemies of Israel from the Land (fulfilled in the Arab-Israeli wars of 1948 and 1967) to allow the Jews to regain and dwell in their homeland again after worldwide dispersion. During this regathering process the Lord said He would return!

"For thus says the Lord: 'Against all My evil neighbors who touch the inheritance which I caused My people Israel to inherit — behold, I will pluck them out of their land and pluck out the house of Judah from among them. Then it shall be, after I have plucked them out, that I will return and have compassion on them and bring them back, everyone to his heritage and everyone to his land'" (*Jeremiah 12:15–16*). See also the Authorized Version of *Deuteronomy 30:1–3* for the same prophecy.

While we were talking with this man, a middle-aged Jewish lady from England heard our conversation and came over to listen to the discussion. She asked me what the phrase on the front of my T-shirt meant, which was a quotation from

Romans 11:18: "You do not support the root, but the root supports you." I told her that this phrase was a verse from the New Testament teaching that Gentile Christians do not take precedence over and above Israel but rather are supported and nurtured by what God has done through Israel. She listened to us and read from the Scriptures in *Jeremiah 31:35–37* where God promised that He would preserve the nation of Israel forever. From that same chapter, we showed her that He would make "a new covenant" (B'rit Hadashah in Hebrew) with Israel (*Jeremiah 31:31–34*) and how it was ratified through the atoning death of Jesus the Messiah *(see Matthew 26:27–28)*. She was interested in learning more, so we left her a Gospel tract that gave steps to accepting this crucified and risen Messiah.

✝ ✢ ✝ ✢ ✝ ✢ ✝

The Holy Spirit led us to a bus stop where we witnessed to an elderly Jewish lady who could not speak English well. A young Israeli teenager heard us, came over to listen, and ended up helping translate for us so that the lady could fully understand the Gospel message from the B'rit Hadashah. This was simply amazing! Without hesitation this young man was willing to help us communicate the Gospel in Hebrew to a fellow countryman. We told them that if they would study the prophecies of the Messiah in the Tanach (our Old Testament) and see how Yeshua fulfilled them in the B'rit Hadashah, they both would come to the obvious conclusion that He is truly the Messiah of Israel come to restore and redeem the Jewish people. Our translator seemed to be more open to the Gospel and so we offered him a copy of a New Testament in Hebrew.

When he took it, the elderly lady began raising her voice. I thought she was angered by our attempt to 'proselytize.' But the young man said that she simply wanted a copy of the New Testament for herself. Unfortunately, I had only one copy because we had already given out the rest. I knew I had only one Hebrew New Testament left; I had checked my bag twice. I was sure of this. So, I expressed my apologies to the lady for not having a copy for her. As we turned to go, I checked my bag for the third and final time. To my shock and utter surprise, sitting right there on top of my tracts was one copy of the Hebrew New Testament, where surely there was none before! If God can easily multiply loaves and fishes out of thin air, why could He not produce a Hebrew New Testament for a sweet and sincere woman who wanted to know the truth? What joy and awe we had at this! I gave her the Scriptures and she thanked me. I have called this event "The Miracle of Replenishment."

A tract of farm land near Qiryat Shimona

✝ ✿ ✝ ✿ ✝ ✿ ✝

The Holy Spirit led us to travel to Qiryat Shimona, a northern city in Israel that borders Lebanon. The terrorist group Hizbollah often victimizes this harmless Jewish community by firing missiles over from the Lebanese border. While at Qiryat Shimona, the Lord guided us to witness to a young lady who was working in a lottery booth. We had asked her directions to an internet café. This encounter opened a door to witness about Jesus being the Jewish Messiah. We told her the fact that the God of Israel created the Chosen People so He could reveal His saving power and love to the world through the greatest Jew of all, Yeshua of Nazareth. She listened with interest and was so grateful for our Gospel witness to her that she kept saying, "Thank you, thank you for telling me about God's love," and blew kisses of appreciation at us. We gave her a Jewish Gospel tract and an Old and New Testament Bible in Hebrew and suggested to her that she read about the wonderful story of what Yeshua has done in bringing God's redemptive love to the Jewish people and the world.

✝ ✡ ✝ ✡ ✝ ✡ ✝

In Galilee as we walked to our car in the parking lot, I looked to my right and spotted the Caesar Hotel. The Spirit quickened me that we should go in to witness to someone. We went into the hotel restaurant and ordered lunch. This move proved to be a divine appointment of God.

We struck up a conversation with our waitress and began sharing with her how the existence of the Jewish people in the world has blessed all of humanity through the eternal covenant of Abraham as foretold in *Genesis 12:1–3*. Building upon that foundation, we further said that the greatest blessing the Jews gave to the world was Yeshua the Messiah, and the Jewish writers of the B'rit Hadashah (New Testament) documented all this. We offered her a free copy of the New Testament in Hebrew.

She was surprised and visibly touched that we would give such an expensive-looking book for free. The young waitress assured us that she would read and study it.

✝ ✡ ✝ ✡ ✝ ✡ ✝

Afterwards, on our way to the Ramat Rachel Kibbutz in Jerusalem, we stopped at a mini-mart to ask for directions and witnessed to three middle-aged Jewish men about Israel's prophetic destiny and the Messiah. They received this and took three copies of the New Testament in Hebrew from us.

✝ ✡ ✝ ✡ ✝ ✡ ✝

Later that day while walking to the Western Wall for prayer, we felt compelled to talk with two Orthodox Jews about the restoration of the Jewish people to Israel as a sign of the Messiah's return. They seemed to agree that the rebirth of Israel in 1948 was a fulfillment of Bible prophecy and that the Messiah was coming soon. The two young men asked if we were Jewish. We answered that we were Jewish in our hearts, circumcised by God's Spirit as promised by Adonai in the New Covenant from *Jeremiah 31:31–34.*

Todd speaks with two young Orthodox Jews

✝ ✡ ✝ ✡ ✝ ✡ ✝

In the afternoon on the same day, the Lord afforded another witnessing opportunity, this time to an owner of a restaurant. She was a Russian immigrant who had come to Israel several years before. We talked with her about how the Jewish Scriptures predicted in *Jeremiah 16 and 23* that at "the end of days" God would bring the Jewish people back into the Land from the "far north" country of Russia. We ended the conversation by concluding that God is regathering the Jews to prepare His people for the return of the Messiah.

Our last day in Jerusalem was spent looking for a Hebrew language computer program. We came to one shop and found out that the manager was into the New Age Movement and Astrology.

I spoke with her about how the prophetic Scriptures in the Tanach (Old Testament) foretold the history of the Jewish people, including their restoration from dispersion to be born a nation again in 1948. I related to her that this partial regathering back into the Promised Land in unbelief (*Ezekiel 20 and 37*) is a sign and indication that the Messiah is soon to return. I deliberately used the word "return" with her because I declared that the Messiah had come before in the person of Jesus of Nazareth, showing her proof of this from a list of the major messianic prophecies given in the Tanach and their corresponding fulfillments in the B'rit Hadashah. She listened with interest and we left her a Messianic prophecy list and Hebrew New Testament.

The Garden of Gethsemane

⁷ And I will establish My covenant between Me and you and your descendants after you in their generations, for an everlasting covenant, to be God to you and your descendants after you. ⁸ Also I give to you and your descendants after you the land in which you are a stranger, all the land of Canaan, as an everlasting possession; and I will be their God."

Genesis 17:7-8

CHAPTER 7

Proclaiming the Messiah

April 2003 - *Todd's fifth mission trip to Israel, this time accompanied by Robert Cuccia*

Each new Gospel outreach in Israel means new challenges rich with new witnessing opportunities - a time for ministry to Israel, a time to see God's providence and power revealed there - a time to proclaim the risen glory of Yeshua the Messiah.

Our outreach of April 2003 was thankfully no different in this regard as we began on the airplane destined for Tel Aviv. On our way from London to Tel Aviv, Robert and I sat next to a Jewish man from London. His name was Brian. Brian told us that his father was Jewish and his mother a Gentile. He converted to Judaism some thirty years ago. He also fought in the Yom Kippur War of 1973. From talking with Brian, we knew he was a very angry and hurting man. He told us his wife died just six months earlier. It was obvious he was still going through the stages of grief. We then witnessed to Him how Jesus can fill the emptiness of his heart with His power, love, and peace. But we further said none of us could earn or be good enough for God, that it was only His grace and mercy that can save us from our sinful selves.

Brian with Todd outside the Tel Aviv airport

The God of Israel did this by providing the ultimate sacrifice for our sins through the sufferings and death of Israel's Messiah as foretold in Isaiah 53 and accurately fulfilled by Jesus at His trial and death. Brian's anger was calmed, as he seemed touched by this message of God's love. He then accepted a Messianic Gospel tract and we concluded our witness to him by saying to him that the Messiah could fill his sorrow with joy, his emptiness of being alone with Messiah's abiding presence giving true purpose and meaning to life. He thanked us for these words and promised to read the Gospel tract showing how one can be saved. Please pray for this man that He will have such an encounter with the Man from Galilee.

✝ ✡ ✝ ✡ ✝ ✡ ✝

We had positive and powerful witnessing encounters in Tel Aviv. Robert and I went into a music store and talked to a young Jewish man named Ori (which means in Hebrew "my light"). I was looking for Handel's Messiah on CD because I accidentally left mine at home. This young man was 22 years old, had an excellent knowledge of classical music, and said

Ori listens intently as Todd witnesses to him.

he loved Handel's great masterpiece. He told us his favorite song in the Oratorio was "And He shall purify the sons of Levi" from Malachi 3:3. This allowed an open door for us to share with him why Yeshua is the Messiah of Israel and how He fulfilled these Biblical prophecies in His life, death, and resurrection that were sung in Handel's Messiah. We said these Messianic prophecies mark and identify who the real Messiah would be. Our focus was on the prophecies which foretold that the Messiah would be pierced in His atoning death. Thus we showed Ori from the Hebrew text the prophecies about this in *Psalm 22:16, Isaiah 53:5-8, Zechariah 12:10* and their fulfillment in Yeshua's death on the cross in *John 19:7*. Ori was amazed.

We offered him a Hebrew New Testament and some tracts going into more detail about how Yeshua fulfilled these prophecies as Messiah. This young man was so profoundly grateful for this gift that he said to us, "What you have given me today is invaluably important to me." I responded by telling him that we believers in Yeshua are indebted to the Jewish people for giving us the Scriptures and the Messiah. His reply blew us away leaving us astonished and surprised. He said "It is I who will be forever in your debt for these things you brought to me today."

I was almost in tears and moved beyond words at this witnessing encounter. Ori's overwhelming gratitude for receiving the Word of God reminded me of when Jesus marveled at the great faith unexpectedly shown by the Gentile centurion in Matthew's Gospel *(Matt. 8:5-10)*. Similarly, in all my nineteen years of witnessing for Christ in the U.S., I have seldom found such overwhelming gratitude shown for receiving the Scriptures by American Christians as Ori expressed when we gave him the Word of God!

✝ ✡ ✝ ✡ ✝ ✡ ✝

On the same day, we stopped at a mini-mart and pool hall to buy soft drinks. In the course of our purchase, we ended up talking to a young lady working there. Her name was

Moran. Robert and I shared with her how the Jewish Messiah of Israel is the central person of Jewish history and Bible prophecy that binds the Tanach (Old Testament) and the B'rit Hadashah (New Testament) together. When we offered her a

Moran (center) enjoys her time with Robert and Todd.

free copy of a Hebrew New Testament, she excitedly exclaimed, "I have always wanted to read this book, but could not find it." We joyfully responded by saying to her that God obviously arranged this very moment as a divine appointment. Now she could read for herself about Israel's true King and real Messiah as truthfully documented in the New Testament. We also gave her a "Prophesied Messiah" bookmark provided by Zola Levitt Ministries that lists all the major Messianic prophecies that were fulfilled by Jesus of Nazareth.

✝ ✡ ✝ ✡ ✝ ✡ ✝

The next day in Tel Aviv, while walking the streets, Robert wanted to stop in a bakery he spotted to buy a pastry or two. During his purchase, we started a conversation with the owner (whose name was Ezekiel) about the restoration and regathering of the Jewish people back into the land of Israel as a major fulfillment of End-Time prophecy and a sign of

Messiah's soon return. We showed him these prophecies from Deuteronomy 30:1-13, and Amos 9:14-15 in the Hebrew text. He also read the great prophecy of Isaiah 66:7-9 about Israel becoming a nation again in one day after going through great travail and suffering. This prophecy was amazingly fulfilled with modern day Israel being declared and born a nation in one day, May 14, 1948, just after the Jews experienced the unspeakable horrors of the Holocaust a few years earlier!

Initially Ezekiel seemed irritated and uninterested when we first came in. But as the Holy Spirit began to open his eyes, his whole countenance changed and he was beaming with excitement. We then went on to say to him that the prophecies of Israel's restoration and regathering was just one stream of Bible prophecy that has been accurately foretold and fulfilled by God to the letter. We said that the other major field of prophecy in the Jewish Scriptures is the prophecies about the Messiah, called Messianic prophecy. Naturally, from that point on in our witness to Ezekiel, we focused on Jesus of Nazareth as being the Person who fulfilled many of those prophecies when He came the first time and will complete the rest of them when He returns. We asked Ezekiel if he wanted to study and know more about Jesus being the Messiah by reading the B'rit Hadashah and

Todd looks with Ezekiel at Scriptures about who the Messiah is and the regathering of Israel in the last days.

the prophecies about Him in the Tanach. He answered with an enthusiastic "yes," so we gave him a Hebrew Bible containing the Old and New Testaments with a list of the major Messianic prophecies Yeshua fulfilled. What a thrill it was to see this man transform with joy and interest at the good news of Israel's Messiah. In September, we plan to follow up and see if at that time he will make a decision to believe in Jesus the Messiah.

"Oh, the depths of the riches both of the wisdom and knowledge of God! How unsearchable are His judgments and His ways past finding out" (Romans *11:33).* God is opening the eyes of Israel slowly to the pierced One they have long rejected which means His coming is near, for the veil is being lifted from Israel's eyes *(2 Cor. 3:15-16).* Truly God is preparing the Chosen People for His return in these last days as evidenced by our witnessing encounters.

✟ ✧ ✟ ✧ ✟ ✧ ✟

Our first witnessing encounter in Tiberias took place in a fishing supply shop. How appropriate was this, I thought, since Jesus said in Matthew 4:19: "*I will make you fishers*

Yehudah, owner of a fishing supply shop accepted a Messianic Gospel tract, but not a B'rit Hadashah

of men." This is exactly what we were doing in Israel. The owner of the shop was named Yehudah. Initially our conversation with him was about the unexpected increase in rainfall for the Galilee region this year after suffering a severe drought for over three years. The lake of Galilee rose twelve feet, he told us, as a result of the much-needed rain. From that point on in the conversation, Robert and I told him the reason why we came to Israel. It was to encourage the Jewish people that the God of Israel will surely complete and fulfill His plan for them as decreed through the biblical Covenants and made central in the Messiah's first and second advent to Israel. The return of the Jewish people back into the land of Israel is a Messianic sign foretold by Moses and the prophets that the Lord will return to them to establish His kingdom on earth *(Deut 30:1-3; Jer. 12:14-15; Is. 11:10-12).*

Yehudah listened as if he were tolerating us, but on the positive side, he did accept a Messianic Gospel tract in the end going into further detail about what we shared with him. He did admonish us to be careful about what we were saying because in some areas of Israel, openly proclaiming Yeshua as Messiah is not tolerated. But we must do so regardless; and in keeping with what the Apostle Peter said in Acts 5:29 when charged not to preach Jesus among the Jewish people anymore, our response must be: "We ought to obey God rather than men."

✝ ✣ ✝ ✣ ✝ ✣ ✝

Next, we went two blocks up and felt led of the Spirit to enter a tourist information center. Once inside, Robert and I met a Jewish lady at the information desk. Her name was Katrina. Our conversation and Gospel witness to her was extensive and lengthy. Working with tourism this lady had pretty much heard of everything under the sun from tourists visiting from all over the world. Therefore our approach had to be memorable and unique from all the things she has heard before. Her view of the Bible - both the Tanach (Old Testament) and B'rit Hadashah (New Testament) was somewhat New Age and egalitarian in that she believed all religious books of the major World Religions are equally valid and true. She alluded to the Kabala (a set of Jewish mystical occult writings of the Middle Ages) placing it on equal level with the Bible. Our answer was that the Bible authenticates itself as being inspired by God and is superior in scope and content to any other religious literary rival. It has been proven through manuscript evidence and transmission, fulfilled prophecy about Messiah and Israel, and archaeology. All of these taken together in their cumulative force have indisputably verified the Bible true in all the claims it makes. We further asserted that the gospel records include credible eyewitness accounts of the life, death, and resurrection of Jesus the Messiah. They are accepted as admissible evidence in any competent court of law (see the book *"The Testimony of the Evangelists"* written by noted lawyer and eminent jurisprudence Scholar Simon Greenleaf).

We challenged her to look at the evidence for herself by reading the New Testament. She affirmed that she would and gladly accepted a Hebrew New Testament and a Messianic Gospel tract. She told us she would read both. Before leaving

Todd explains to Katrina why the Bible isn't just another religious book.

her, we concluded our conversation by telling her that, if she had doubts about the truth of Jesus being the Messiah, she should try a simple experiment: when she is at the end of her rope to call on Yeshua in the day of trouble and He will answer her and prove that He is who He claims to be - Lord and Messiah. If she did this with a sincere, seeking, and open heart, she will not be disappointed but will personally verify and discover this truth. God's Word promises this very thing. *"**Call upon Me in the day of trouble. I will deliver you, and you shall glorify Me. Call to Me, and I will answer you, and show you great and mighty things, which you do not know**"* (Psalm 50:15; Jeremiah 33:3).

Later that day, we drove to a place on the northern shore of the lake of Galilee where Jesus restored Peter in *John 21* and where Jesus performed 18 of His 33 miracles in and around that area. While Robert and I were looking out on the waters of Galilee, two young Jewish men approached us and asked us what happened at this place. Robert and I proceeded to tell them about the great events written in the 21st chapter of the Gospel of John. From that brief Bible lesson and witness about the resurrection of Yeshua the Messiah, one of the young men wanted to engage in a controversial political discussion about Israel, the Arabs and the whole Middle East crises involved with it. At this point, it was more of a monologue with this young man wanting to hear himself attempt to wax eloquent. He rambled on about how Israel (believe it or not!) was the real terrorist state and the Arabs were the innocent victims from the beginning of the conflict. He even went so far as to say, against Scripture, history, and archaeology, the Arabs lived in the land long before the Jews lived there and they should give more land away to the Palestinian Arabs to bring about peace (contra the failed Oslo Peace Accords which brought more terrorism and death to Israel afterwards than any time before!). Sadly, this young man's myopic perspective seems to have blinded him to the dangerous realities of Israel's threatened existence in the Middle East. The very nation he falsely accused in our hearing of being no better than the Arab dictatorships around it actually is the only nation in that region that guarantees his democratic rights to speak out against the state of Israel. I believe he has been hoodwinked by the radical left in Israel whom he was parroting, and also by the Arab fifth column working undercover in Israel against Israel by dividing the Jews against each other over the current Middle East crisis.

In his political naiveté and detached idealism, this young man thought dictators like Arafat and all the other dictators of the Arab world could easily be appeased by giving into their demands. But we obligingly pointed out to this person that history has repeatedly taught us that dictators and tyrants simply cannot be appeased; therefore it has been and will be no different with Arab dictators of the likes of Arafat, Hussein, Assad, and others. We firmly and calmly told him that he was dead wrong in his wild assertions; that the Scriptures, history, and the plain facts of the case as they stand, clearly refute his ridiculous and absurd claims made against his own country. Any patriotic Jew of Israel would have rightly considered his insane denunciations made

Todd with Judas and his friend, the two of whom have been deceived about the Middle East crisis.

against the Jewish State of Israel treasonous and this person a "meshumed" (Hebrew for "traitor"). As a chilling conclusion to this unpleasant affair, when we parted company from this man and his friend, the young man told us his name - he said: "My name is Judas!"

Pray that this Judas will not meet the same horrible end as Judas of old did in his treachery. Ask God to open his blind eyes to the great truths of Yeshua and God's unconditional love for and defense of Israel (see Isaiah 54:17; Jeremiah 33:3), lest this person find himself opposing God and losing his own soul in eternal perdition.

✝ ✡ ✝ ✡ ✝ ✡ ✝

On April 16, the sixth day of our Gospel outreach in Israel, Robert Cuccia and I visited a family that I witnessed to and developed a close friendship with on a prior trip. The mother and father's names are Tamar and Yoram and the names of their three children (triplets consisting of two sons and one daughter) are Dana, Noam, and Ophir. They invited us to stay at their house and celebrate the Passover with them and their family. Passover of course is one of the seven feasts of Israel celebrated every year by the people of Israel. It

Yoram, Tamar, and Todd with three unhappy triplets
at Todd and Robert's departure

commemorates the Exodus when God delivered the Jewish people from bondage and slavery in Egypt some 3,500 years ago. The Lord gave Robert and me opportunities among Tamar, Yoram, and their family members to explain how the elements of the Passover meal are a type and shadow of Yeshua the Messiah in His atoning death as the lamb of God. In addition to having the Passover Haggadah (the liturgical instruction manual for the order of celebrating the Passover) in English for Pesach, I also brought a book on the Passover written from a Messianic Jewish perspective that showed how Jesus the Messiah fulfilled Passover and the other feasts of Israel. Tamar's brother David took an interest in the book and I explained that the premise of the book was to show how the seven feasts of Israel are prophetic and point to the person and work of the Messiah. David turned to Robert later during the Passover meal and mentioned the fact that part of the prayers said during the Passover meal is for the Jews to be regathered back into the land of Israel to await the coming of the Messiah.

Robert responded by telling him that this is exactly what God is currently doing by bringing the Jews back to the land

Todd and Robert were blessed with the opportunity to celebrate a traditional Passover with the whole family.

in this day—a sure sign that the Messiah is soon to return! After everyone left the house, Tamar and I cleaned the house until three in the morning. During this time Tamar asked me if I felt God's presence there. I enthusiastically said, "Yes!" She replied, "I wish I could experience that, too." I told her she could by accepting Yeshua into her heart and believing He is the atoning Messiah for her sins. "When this is done, God will fill you with the Ruach Hakodesh (Hebrew for "Holy Spirit")." I further said to her that Yeshua promised in His Word to give God's Holy Spirit to those who simply ask in childlike faith. For if she, an imperfect person and mother, gives what is good to her children, how much more will God, who is perfect, give the gift of the Holy Spirit to those who believe in Yeshua (Luke 11:9-13). She listened attentively and I later read to her what Jesus said about the process of regeneration and the necessity of spiritual rebirth (being born-again) in Him from John chapter 3. I concluded this biblical discourse by informing Tamar that all these things were written and foretold in the Jewish Scriptures. God told Israel He would make a New Covenant with them wherein He would give the covenanted nation a new heart and put His Spirit within them (Ezekiel 36:25-27). Dear readers, please pray for Tamar and her family. She is not far from the kingdom of God and is close to accepting Yeshua as her Messiah.

✝ ✡ ✝ ✡ ✝ ✡ ✝

A day later, back in Tiberias, Robert and I decided to visit the Caesar Hotel for a cappuccino. Our waiter was eager to listen about Israel's supernatural history, guided and directed by the power and providence of a sovereign God, from Abraham to the present time. We told this young man, whose name was Zyion (in English that translates to Zion), that God chose to reveal Himself through the Jewish people to the world by the Holy Scriptures which they wrote. These writings culminate in the coming of Yeshua the Messiah whose life and ministry were written and recorded by Jews in the New Testament. We also emphasized that God has promised to preserve Israel as a nation forever. No other ethnic nation can claim such a promise from Scripture (Jeremiah 31:35-37). Zyion listened with sincere interest and eagerly accepted a Hebrew copy of the Old and New Testaments.

This young waiter, Zyion, eagerly
accepted a Hebrew copy of the Bible

After he took the copy of the Scriptures, he came back to our table and was surprised that the New Testament Scriptures were written in Hebrew. We told him that it was written in the original language of Israel because Jesus was Jewish, the first Christians were Jews, and the first "church" was in Jerusalem. Thus, the New Testament would naturally be originally written in Hebrew reflecting the people, land, and culture it came from. He was very open to our Gospel witness for Christ.

✝ ✡ ✝ ✡ ✝ ✡ ✝

Several days later, we arrived in Jerusalem and on Resurrection Sunday (in the West, it is called Easter by mainline denominational churches) went out to proclaim to the Jewish people there that, on this day, mankind's greatest enemy, Death, was conquered by the Prince of Life when

He came out of the tomb in the city of Jerusalem 2,000 years ago. This epochal event of human history is extremely relevant to every human being because death happens to us all and we need a real answer to this universal enemy of life — that answer is exclusively found in the risen Christ! After prayer for God's anointing to boldly proclaim this message in Jerusalem and His guidance in leading our steps on the right path, we hit the streets of Jerusalem near our hotel to proclaim the good news of Yeshua the Messiah risen from the dead.

Our first witnessing encounter took place when we stopped to ask an elderly Jewish man for directions to a certain section of the city. He was sitting on a park bench reading a newspaper. His name was Joseph. Joseph patiently listened to us as we told him about what happened on this Sunday in the city of Jerusalem two thousand years ago. The Messiah died for our sins and the God of Israel raised Him from the dead to signify that Jesus was the unique Son of God. His payment for Israel's and the world's sins was approved by the Father, which gives ultimate victory over death to those who believe in Him *(Romans 1:1-4; 2 Timothy 1:10)*. Joseph said he had a problem with the existence of God because of the holocaust and the gratuitous amount of

Joseph said he didn't believe in God because of the evil in the world.

evil in the world. Our reply was that we understood why he felt that way but that evil exists not because God does not exist, but rather man being a free moral agent and given the gift of free will chose to disobey God from the beginning. This in turn brought the negative consequences (pain, suffering, evil, and death) of that disobedience on all creation and human posterity (See *Genesis 2 and Romans 5*). God originally endowed man with a free will so that he would love his Creator by choice, not by force or coercion. This naturally involved a risk that man would choose to do wrong. The present reason for the existence of evil is because each of us is born with a natural tendency toward evil ("the evil inclination" as the rabbis call it); and it is this inward evil from which we need a Savior to save us.

We further shared with Joseph the good news that God so loved Israel and the world that He sent His Son to be our Savior and Messiah to deliver us from the evil within us and without us. The resurrection of Yeshua from the dead is God's guarantee that death and sin will finally be destroyed. Joseph agreed with this line of reasoning in principle. We gave him a Hebrew New Testament to read and a Gospel tract in Hebrew too. He politely thanked us and left when his girlfriend arrived. Pray that our sharing the Gospel truth will take root and bear fruit and produce faith in the Messiah in his life.

✞ ✠ ✞ ✠ ✞ ✠ ✞

As we continued our witness for the risen Savior in Jerusalem, I noticed a Jewish New Age bookstore down near the end of the street we were walking. I felt compelled by the Holy Spirit to go inside there and talk to the owner. The owner's name was Yacov (Jacob in English). His bookstore contained books on every major world religion (Islam, Judaism, Hinduism, Buddhism, etc.) and the occult. The glaring omission from his eclectic selection was Biblical Christianity. Jacob was intelligent about each world religion. His belief system was therefore pluralistic. He took the more positive truths from each of these major religions to comprise one of his own making. One of the problems with this eclectic approach, we humbly conveyed to him, was that it ignores the irreconcilable differences that clearly exist between Christianity and the rest of the world's religions. The founders of these other major religions never made the claims Jesus

Robert with Yacov (Jacob), the owner of a Jewish New Age bookstore

made about Himself, be it Buddha, Muhammad, Confucius, and others. Jesus pointedly claimed to be God and the Messiah *(John 8:58-59; Mark 15:61-62)*. The truthfulness of these astounding claims all hinged on whether Christ rose from the dead. We further told Jacob that He did in fact rise from the dead and through this alone brought the answer to the problem of death.

The historic event of the resurrection makes Jesus far superior to any other spiritual or religious leader in the history of the world. No other religion or its many founders and leaders did what Jesus did in defeating death for all mankind. With all his intellectual knowledge of philosophy and religion, Jacob could not give us a credible response to this partly due to his unbelief and the profound simplicity of our argument. We thanked Jacob for his time. He was open to receive two Gospel tracts from us. Dear readers, please pray that the Holy Spirit of God will enlighten Jacob's mind and heart to see that Yeshua alone is the perfect and exclusive revelation of God to man and that in the Messiah are all the treasures of wisdom and knowledge *(Colossians 2:3)*.

✝ ✡ ✝ ✡ ✝ ✡ ✝

Shortly after departing from there, Robert spotted a shop that sold coffee and wine and wanted to go in. This seemingly unimportant incident no doubt was arranged by the providence of God so that we could have an effective witness about the risen Messiah to an open soul. As we entered the store, I mentioned to Robert that I had been to Napa Valley, California, several times before to enjoy the beauty of its landscape. Napa Valley is also known for being the wine country of California. A Jewish man from America overheard me and immediately came up to me and told me he lived in Mendocino, California. His name was Alan Stein. We told him that we visit Israel twice a year to proclaim the Good News of Yeshua the Messiah.

We told Alan that it was on this day (Resurrection Sunday) that the epochal event of history occurred in Jerusalem. He knew we were talking about the resurrection of Jesus. We further said the evidence that Jesus was the

Alan, from Mendocino, California, listened intently to the Gospel.

Messiah of Israel was based on the many Messianic prophecies He fulfilled and His resurrection from the dead. Alan gladly listened to us and was very open to our Gospel witness. He took the "Prophesied Messiah" bookmark that lists the major Old Testament prophecies of Messiah and their direct fulfillment by Jesus in the New Testament. Alan enthusiastically said he would look these prophecies up in a New Testament he owned. We then gave our own personal testimonies of how Yeshua changed our lives by His great love, forgiveness, and transforming power through faith in Him. We told him that one significant example of this transformation is seen by the supernatural love He placed in our hearts for the Jewish people. Pray God's Spirit will draw Alan to Yeshua in love and truth.

☥ ✡ ☥ ✡ ☥ ✡ ☥

The next day, we walked down Ben Yehudah Street. This street is the most famous in Israel and Jerusalem for its many shops. In one gift shop we talked to a young Israeli man named Aaron. He was open to our Gospel witness about Jesus the Messiah. When we offered him a B'rit Hadashah (Hebrew New Testament), he exclaimed with surprise, "You would give

Aaron was appreciative of the New Testament given to him

that to me?" He was very appreciative. We left him Bible literature listing the prophecies given about the Messiah in the Jewish Bible so that he could look them up in the B'rit Hadashah and see how Yeshua fulfilled them.

✝ ✡ ✝ ✡ ✝ ✡ ✝

We got back to our hotel at 9:30 P.M.. The night clerk greeted us. She was there to check us in the first day we arrived at the hotel in Jerusalem. Robert had a book with him entitled *The Messiah of the Tanach, Targums, and Talmuds.*

She inquired about it. Naturally, or should I say supernaturally, that led Robert and me to witness to her about Yeshua the Messiah of Israel. We said the book quoted the interpretations of the ancient rabbis about the Messiah found in the verses of the Tanach and how they actually applied to Yeshua of Nazareth as documented in the B'rit Hadashah. She listened as we explained one of the many Messianic prophecies Yeshua fulfilled when He came to Israel the first time. The prophecy we showed her to read was Isaiah 53 and how that was exactly fulfilled in the sufferings and vicarious death of Yeshua. She read that entire chapter with

The night clerk at the hotel reads Isaiah 53 for the first time

us and then read the corresponding fulfillment found in Acts 8:26-40. She read both biblical texts in Hebrew. We told her that this prophecy was just one of many Yeshua fulfilled at His first coming and that when He returns to Israel again soon He will completely fulfill the rest of the prophecies that pertain to the second coming of the Messiah and thereby complete God's program for the Jewish people.

✝ ✡ ✝ ✡ ✝ ✡ ✝

On the morning of April 22, our Gospel witness began at CaCao Restaurant with our waitress whose name was Leora. Robert and I simply expressed our sincere and deep gratitude for what her people gave to us — the Bible, Yeshua the Messiah, and the Judeo-Christian ethic by which most of Western civilization was greatly influenced and governed. We further elaborated that it is the Messiah who is the crowning achievement of the Jewish people. He is the central Person that unites the Tanach and the B'rit Hadashah together. She marveled at what we said and remarked that this was all new to her. We went on to inform her that Jesus is the Messiah of her people by virtue of the fact that He fulfilled

Waitress, Leora, gladly accepted a B'rit Hadashah

those specific prophecies made about the Messiah in the Jewish Bible (Tanach) through His epochal life, death, and resurrection. She gladly accepted the B'rit Hadashah (Jewish New Testament) from us and said she would read it.

✝ ✧ ✝ ✧ ✝ ✧ ✝

The next witnessing encounter that day tested our resolve (particularly mine) to preach God's love for the unlovable. The person I am referring to was an Arab man who was the attendant at the entrance to the Church of Gallicantu, the site where Peter denied Jesus three times and where Christ stood on trial before Caiphas the High Priest in his palace. The Arab man was responsible for collecting the nominal fee required for entering this genuine Holy site. In our conversation with him, the Middle East crisis between Israel and the Arabs came up. Both he and an elderly British man sitting in the booth with him went absolutely ballistic when we casually mentioned that God is restoring the Jewish people to their ancient homeland as the Bible precisely predicted beforehand. Both of these men, especially the Arab

The Holy Spirit filled Robert with God's love to calm a hostile situation

man, began spouting the most loathsome anti-Semitic vitriol against the Jewish people. They accused both America and Israel of being Terrorist States against the Arab world. In my mind, I was so utterly appalled and enraged that I wanted to vociferously denounce them as vile anti-Semitic liars. But Robert took the lead by patiently explaining to them that only the supernatural love of God revealed through Jesus the Messiah can bring positive change in the individual and, by outward extension, permanent peace to the Middle East.

It was at this specific point that the Lord was testing my faithfulness to His teaching about loving one's enemies. My natural inclinations wanted to blast and verbally excoriate both of these hate-filled men. But I found the Holy Spirit sovereignly intervened and took control of my mind and heart on this matter. Softly, yet firmly, I reiterated what Robert said about God's love for them as revealed through the Gospel freely given to all, both Jew and Arab, so that Messiah can unite them as one, which He will do perfectly when He returns. What Robert had eloquently said quelled their anger into attentive silence as they listened to the unique message of the Gospel he and I proclaimed.

I reinforced Robert's witness with my personal testimony of how Christ's great love transformed me, once a violent, antipathetic atheist and hater of God and those who believed in Jesus Christ, into a faithful servant who wants to humbly share that love with a world in dire need. Jesus said all true followers of His are to love their enemies and bless those who curse them (Matthew 5:44). Robert and I did just that, but only by the power of the Spirit of God's supernatural grace. The best way for Christians to love the unlovable is by showing the character of Christ's love in both word and deed. We did this by giving them the Gospel. Our witness silenced the voice of the enemy speaking through them so much so that Robert was able to give this Arab man a New Testament to read in Hebrew! Quite amazing is the power of God's love!

✝ ✿ ✝ ✿ ✝ ✿ ✝

Later that afternoon, I decided to buy an ice cream in the Jewish quarter of Jerusalem. We shared with the owner and his family that the God of Israel has not forgotten the promises and covenants He has made with their people Israel. These promises, contained in the covenants, find their fulfillment and blessing through the person and work of the Messiah whom we proclaim to be Yeshua. They heartily thanked us for our support and received a Gospel tract about why Jesus is the Messiah of Israel.

This Jewish family accepted a Gospel tract and thanked Robert and Todd for their support of Israel.

✝ ✿ ✝ ✿ ✝ ✿ ✝

When we returned to our hotel at the end of the day, Robert went downstairs and talked to the desk clerk who was at the front desk. Robert witnessed to her about the case for Jesus being the Messiah through the fulfillment of prophecies given in the Jewish Scriptures. He challenged her to read the New Testament and see for herself. I then came downstairs and offered her a complete Bible in Hebrew containing both the Old and New Testaments. She received it and a tract that has these prophecies and where they are found in the Scriptures.

✝ ✡ ✝ ✡ ✝ ✡ ✝

The next day was sadly the day of our departure from Israel. We had to take a taxi from Jerusalem to the airport in Tel Aviv because our rental car was locked up in a public garage that would not open up until the day after we left. Needless to say I was very upset and in my limited and self-centered perspective I began wondering why the Lord allowed this trying circumstance to occur. Ah, but God says in His Word, *"My thoughts are not your thoughts, nor My ways your ways, says the Lord"* (Isaiah 55:8-9). The Lord allowed this significant inconvenience to happen so that we could witness to our taxi driver on the way to the airport.

She was a middle-aged woman. Her name was Ety. We told her that we were grateful for the gift of the Messiah and the Scriptures the Jewish people gave the Gentile world. She was happy to hear this and when we reached our destination, we were able to give her a Hebrew New Testament and materials about Jesus being the Messiah. We would not have been able to share the Messiah with her had our car not been inaccessible. God allowed this misfortune so that she could hear and believe in the good tidings of salvation.

"Lord, forgive me when things do not go my way at times and I think circumstances should be scheduled around my convenience and ease. Often times You allow the inconveniences of life, the inconveniences of difficulty and hardship, to provide an opportunity to serve You, as You did in this particular event."

Lord willing, we are bound again for Israel in November to conduct our sixth Gospel outreach. Like the five Gospel outreaches before, I know the Lord will do *"awesome things we do not expect"* (*Isaiah 64:3*).

³¹ "Behold, the days are coming, says the LORD, when I will make a new covenant with the house of Israel and with the house of Judah— ³² not according to the covenant that I made with their fathers in the day that I took them by the hand to lead them out of the land of Egypt, My covenant which they broke, though I was a husband to them, says the LORD. ³³ But this is the covenant that I will make with the house of Israel after those days, says the LORD: I will put My law in their minds, and write it on their hearts; and I will be their God, and they shall be My people. ³⁴ No more shall every man teach his neighbor, and every man his brother, saying, 'Know the LORD,' for they all shall know Me, from the least of them to the greatest of them, says the LORD. For I will forgive their iniquity, and their sin I will remember no more."

Jeremiah 31:31-34

CHAPTER 8:

Sharing
Good
Tidings

November 2003 - *Todd's sixth mission trip to Israel, accompanied again by Robert Cuccia*

November's Gospel 2003 outreach to the Jewish people of Israel commenced in Jerusalem. We arrived at the Holy City in the late morning of November 4. After a short rest, we drove into the city to begin our witness of Jesus the Messiah to His ethnic people. We parked the car and walked to Ben Yehudah Street—a place always teeming with social activity. Our evangelistic purpose of course, as with all these short-term mission trips, was to share the Gospel of Yeshua Hamashiach (Hebrew for "Jesus the Messiah") to those who would listen and to those to whom the Spirit of God led Robert Cuccia and me to talk about the wonderful Savior of Israel.

Having purposed this in our hearts, we stepped into a jewelry shop and talked to the owner, a man by the name of Rami, about God's pledge to protect and preserve the nation of Israel forever and the fact that He is bound to them through the eternal, immutable, and unconditional covenants He has made with the chosen nation as revealed in the Scriptures.

Rami, the owner of a jewelry store, reads along with Todd about how Jesus is the Messiah

Rami replied by showing us his copy of the Jewish Scriptures (what Christians would call the Old Testament) that he had received while in the army. To verify what we told Rami, Robert and I showed him the great promise God gave Israel in *Jeremiah 31:31-37* guaranteeing their eternal existence and the fact that He would make "a New Covenant" with "the house of Israel". Rami read the text for himself that I showed him in Hebrew. I then showed him from the New Testament (*Matthew 26:28*, to be precise) in Hebrew how Jesus as the Messiah had fulfilled and brought that New Covenant to Israel so that forgiveness of sins could be offered. We offered Rami the inspired and official record of how the Messiah ratified this New Covenant with Israel (and all who believe) by giving him a copy of the New Testament in Hebrew, he could then study for himself to see that such things were true and worthy of reception.

✝ ✡ ✝ ✡ ✝ ✡ ✝

After we left the jewelry store, a young teenage couple immediately approached us and asked us for money. Whether it was wise or not, I gave them $5.00. But such a gesture opened the door for a Gospel witness to them; indeed, we

God led this purpose-seeking young couple to Todd and Robert to hear the Gospel

are willing to spend and be spent so that the crucified and risen Messiah may be proclaimed to Israel. You could tell by looking at this couple that they were searching for a purpose to their lives but were still left unhappy and without answers to the basic questions of life. This led Robert and me to tell them that we too were looking for answers to life's basic questions (questions like: "Why am I here," "What is the meaning of life," Is there a God" and so forth) and found those answers satisfactorily answered in a personal relationship with the God of Israel through His son Yeshua the Messiah. I then felt led to ask if I could pray with them there on the spot. They allowed me to do so and I asked the Lord to reveal His great love for them and convict them of sin and bring them to the Savior. They prayed with us and received a Hebrew New Testament and Messianic Gospel tracts that demonstrate from the Jewish Scriptures why Jesus is the Messiah of the Jewish people.

✝ ✡ ✝ ✡ ✝ ✡ ✝

Several minutes later, two Orthodox Jews who belong to the Chabad Lubavitch movement approached us asking for alms. The names of these two men were David and Moses. This Orthodox sect of Judaism believes that the founder of their movement, the late Rabbi Menachem Schneersohn (1902-1994), was the Messiah! No surprise here, for Jesus predicted that one of the signs in the last days before His return would be people coming in His name falsely claiming to be the Messiah (see *Matthew 24:5, 23-24*). This erroneous belief allowed Robert and me to engage in a conversation with them about the true identity of the Messiah as laid out in the series of Messianic prophecies revealed in the Tanach (The Old Testament). We said to them that the person who fulfilled these prophecies would then be the one true and real Messiah excluding all others, and there was only one Person in Jewish history that has literally fulfilled them to the letter - Yeshua min Nazarit (Jesus of Nazareth), not Rabbi Schneersohn of Brooklyn, New York.

These Orthodox men, David and Moses, asked for alms and received the Truth about the one true Messiah

One obvious prophecy that clearly identifies who this Messiah would be is the prophecy of how He would die and innocently suffer to atone for the sins of Israel and the world and would be physically "pierced" through in the process. We quoted *Isaiah 53:5* and *Psalm 22:16* to them as proof texts. We further pointed out that for this reason and many, many others Schneerson could in no way be the Messiah simply because He did not experience a death caused by piercing that would atone for man's sins, nor did he live a perfect life; all of which Jesus had and did when He walked in Israel some 2,000 years ago. David then made an allusion to *Zechariah 14:4* that when the Messiah comes, it will be at the Mount of Olives just east of Jerusalem. We affirmed that was indeed correct but further showed him and Moses from the same book in *Zechariah 12:10* the prediction that when the Messiah returns to Jerusalem at the Mount of Olives, the Jewish people living at that time will see that this returning Messiah was pierced in His physical body. Indubitably this points to the fact that Messiah came in the person of Jesus who was pierced in crucifixion and will return with these same marks on the body. We quoted to them another amazing prophecy in Zechariah where Israel will recognize the Messiah's pierced wounds in His hands (see *Zechariah 13:6-7*). David and Moses listened and pondered what we said. They blessed us in Hebrew and we were able to give them literature on the other Messianic prophecies found in Scripture and how Jesus alone uniquely fulfilled them by His birth, life, death, and resurrection; something Rebbe Schneersohn did not and could never do in his rabbinical life.

✝ ✡ ✝ ✡ ✝ ✡ ✝

On this amazing Gospel outreach to the Jewish people of Israel, the Lord indeed **"did awesome things we did not expect"** (*Isaiah 64:3*). A powerful example of this very thing happened in Jerusalem while witnessing for the Messiah to the Jewish people living there.

After prayer on the morning of November 5, we felt led by the Spirit of God to go and pray at the Western Wall and then walk through the Jewish quarter of the Old City. Our stop at the Western Wall was undoubtedly a distinct display of the providence of God; for while we were at the Wall praying, an Orthodox Jew approached us to ask if we were Jewish. I told

Robert and Todd were invited to help make a minyan by these Orthodox men in the synagogue next to the Western Wall

him through an interpreter that we were Jewish in our hearts by virtue of the fact that we have Jesus the risen Messiah living in us. He asked us this question because he wanted us to help him make a minyan in the synagogue adjacent to the Western Wall so that he could say formal prayers from the Siddur (the official prayer book of Judaism). A minyan is a group composed of ten men above Bar Mitzvah age (12 years old) and, in Jewish law, is required in order for a prayer or synagogue service to occur. Both Robert and I jumped at this opportunity - we knew that this was a golden opportunity from God by providential arrangement to witness to these Orthodox Jews about why Jesus is the Messiah of Israel.

After the prayer service, one of the Orthodox Jews asked where we came from. When we told them that we lived in Dallas, Texas, one of the men asked me if I knew a certain Rabbi there. I said that I not only knew him well, but also that he comes to visit Jewish patients in the hospital where I am currently working as a chaplain. The other two Orthodox men said they knew this Rabbi as well. One went to Yeshiva school with his son and the other had attended this Rabbi's synagogue when he used to live in Dallas ten years ago! What are the chances that these three men, totally unrelated to each other, as well as I, knew this rabbi?

God obviously arranged this meeting in the Synagogue next to the holiest site in all of Judaism so that the Messiah Jesus could lovingly be shared with them. For the mutual association we shared in knowing this Rabbi allowed Robert and me to relate to them our love for Israel and the Jewish people. We explained how God is regathering them back to their ancient homeland in preparation for the return of the Messiah as foretold by Moses and the Prophets. We then said plainly to them that the Scriptures both from the Tanach (Old Testament) and B'rit Hadashah (New Testament) reveal this Messiah to be none other than Yeshua min Nazarit (Hebrew for "Jesus of Nazareth"). Incredibly, they listened to us without rebuff or visible displeasure as one might expect, but gladly received our testimony concerning Jesus in their own synagogue and received from us Messianic Jewish Gospel tracts giving further explanation and proof from the Jewish Scriptures why Jesus is the Messiah and must be believed in for salvation.

✝ ✡ ✝ ✡ ✝ ✡ ✝

As we were returning to our car that evening, we noticed a man in a wheelchair playing with his puppy. We stopped and petted his small dog and began to share with him about Jesus being the Messiah of Israel. The man's name was Joseph. He was obviously interested in what we were saying. The Ruach Hakodesh (Hebrew for the Holy Spirit) of God was opening Joseph's heart to the Gospel, so much so that he invited us into his house for a deeper conversation.

In the course of our conversation with Joseph, he told us that he had a friend who was a Jewish believer in Jesus the Messiah, and that he had extensively shared with Joseph the same things we were telling him about Messianic prophecy in the Tanach and how they are fulfilled in Yeshua alone. We had an hour-long Bible study with Joseph from both the English and Hebrew texts of the Scriptures. One major

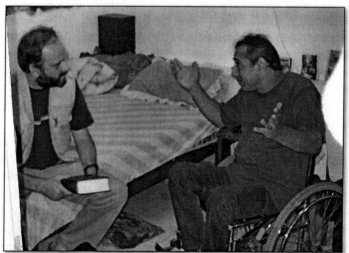

Joseph said he could accept that Jesus is the same as God, and he accepted Jesus as his Savior!

subject of Messianic prophecy we studied with him was the fact the Messiah would be raised from the dead as King David foretold 1,000 years before Jesus was born (*Psalm 16:10-11*) and the corresponding fulfillment by the resurrection of Jesus of Nazareth in *Acts 2:22-36*.

In broken English, Joseph said he could accept that Jesus is the Messiah and was the same as God! Robert and I made sure this is what he said and meant; it was, and we were quite amazed at what the Spirit of God was doing here in bringing this Jewish man to faith in the Messiah of Israel. Robert and I then went over Scriptures that clearly pointed to Jesus as being the only valid way to God and the sole means by which one is saved from the penalty of sin, and the power of hell and death. This salvation consists of believing that Jesus is Adonai (Hebrew for "Lord") and that God raised His Son from the dead to give us life with Him forever (see *John 14:6-7; Isaiah 49:7-8; Romans 10:9-10*).

After this, we went through the plan of salvation as laid out in Paul's New Testament book of Romans known as "The Roman Road of Salvation". When we completed this study with Joseph and made sure he understood this life-giving message of the Gospel, we asked him if he would like to invite Yeshua into his heart as Lord and Messiah to become a fulfilled Jew born anew in Messiah. **Joseph eagerly answered "yes" and prayed with us and was gloriously saved right there on the spot!** He then exclaimed to us several times over "Yeshua Ha Mashiach" (Jesus is the Messiah) and "Yeshua is the same as God."

Needless to say, Robert and I greatly rejoiced with the angels in heaven over this soul who repented and believed in Jesus the Messiah to truly become a son of Abraham. Coming out of Joseph's house after witnessing this miracle of salvation, I thought to myself that if I were unable to go to Israel anymore or my life should abruptly end, it was worth all the arduous toil, long hours of witnessing, and twenty years of hardship, struggle, and studying the Scriptures to see this dear Jewish brother become a child of God through his faith in the Jewish Messiah. Glory to God!

✝ ✡ ✝ ✡ ✝ ✡ ✝

The following morning, Robert and I went to an outlet mall about three miles north of where we were staying. Once we got there, Robert noticed a store where lamps and light fixtures were sold. He told me that he once sold lighting merchandise and so we used this past occupation of his to establish a point of contact with the store manager. This further opened the door to share the Gospel with him.

The manager's name was Asher. In our witness to him, we explained how both the Tanach and the B'rit Hadashah are bound as one in the Messiah Jesus. Just as God gave prophetic signs for His first coming in the Scriptures that were literally fulfilled, so even now God has given the world a sign in Scripture that the Messiah is about to return - the prophetic sign and fulfillment of the Jews' return to their ancient homeland from the Diaspora (*Isaiah 11:11-12*).

Asher replied that he had briefly studied the New Testament in school for only its historical value. We encouraged him to

Asher, the manager of the lamp store, had briefly studied the New Testament in school

study the detailed prophecies of the Messiah as foretold in the Tanach and their accurate fulfillment in the life of Jesus of Nazareth as recorded in the New Testament. We concluded our witness to Asher and his co-worker by saying that Jesus was more than a mere man but was the divine Messiah who conquered death by His resurrection. If someone claiming to be both Lord and Messiah as Jesus proved Himself to be by rising from the dead, we should listen and believe in what He has to say.

We thanked them for their time and left them with a Hebrew New Testament and Gospel tracts so that they could search the matter for themselves and come to the knowledge of the truth. This is exactly what Yeshua commands every person to do in *John 5:39*. ***"Search the Scriptures. For in them you think you have eternal life, and these are they which testify of Me."***

✝ ✿ ✝ ✿ ✝ ✿ ✝

As we continued our witness for Jesus the Messiah in Jerusalem, we came upon a carpenter's shop and looked at some of the custom doors made there. Robert is a carpenter and took a natural interest in what was in the store. The carpenter's name was Galley, and he was open to our witness about the most famous carpenter in the world who we told him was none other than Jesus of Nazareth. We said to him that God inspired the Jewish prophets and men to communicate His revealed word to the world, not only in the Tanach but also equally in the B'rit Hadashah (The New Testament). Robert and I emphasized this especially because the Jewish world has been mistakenly led to believe that only the Tanach is the accepted Word of God. The B'rit Hadashah cannot be accepted because it unabashedly proclaims Yeshua is the Messiah.

We said to Galley that if he would simply study the many prophecies made about the Messiah in the Tanach and then read where they have been fulfilled by Yeshua in the B'rit Hadashah, he would plainly see that the man born in

Bethlehem, raised in Nazareth, crucified and risen in Jerusalem, is none other than Israel's Messiah.

Galley was genuinely grateful that we gave him a Hebrew New Testament and a tract listing the major Messianic prophecies. He replied that he would read it to gain knowledge about this very important subject and further said that he did not want to be ignorant about such things but wanted to know for himself if it was true.

Todd and Robert spoke to Galley, a carpenter, about the most famous carpenter in the world

✝ ✧ ✝ ✧ ✝ ✧ ✝

The next day we departed from Jerusalem, for Tiberias and the region of Galilee where Jesus began His three years of ministry in Israel. Half way between Tiberias and Tel Aviv, we stopped to eat lunch at a pizzeria. After we finished eating we left, but right before we got to the car, Robert realized we forgot to get our receipts. So Robert went back to retrieve them while I pulled the car around to meet him back there.

When I walked into the restaurant again, I found Robert had struck up a conversation with a Jewish family of three. The names of the father and mother were Eric and Na'it. Eric asked us why we came to Israel. Robert and I answered with gentleness and respect that we came to proclaim that God's plan for Israel centrally involves the first and second comings of the Messiah whom the Jewish Scriptures clearly identify as Yeshua of Nazareth. At this point, Eric told us that his wife was a high school teacher. I asked Na'it what she taught and to my surprise she said "Old Testament history!" Upon hearing this, I immediately knew then that this so-called "accidental encounter" was not a mere coincidence. This divine appointment was scheduled by God's providence so that they could know that all the prophets and the Law find their completion and fulfillment in the New Testament.

Na'it did not even own a copy of the New Testament (B'rit Hadashah) in Hebrew, a book written by Jews from cover to cover about a Jewish Messiah living in a Jewish land. It is astounding to me that many Jewish people like Na'it never read the most famous part of the Bible written 2,000 years ago. But through our discussion, she did see the logic in studying the New Testament from the Jewish perspective in which it was written. I then showed her a list of the major prophecies about Messiah in the Hebrew Tanach and where they are fulfilled in the B'rit Hadashah. I told her that

Eric and Na'it were interested in studying the New Testament from the Jewish perspective

I happened to have a free copy to give to her, which she gladly accepted. We then related to her that the prophecies about the Messiah found in the Tanach are defined, clarified, and fulfilled in the greatest Jew who ever lived and is alive today (*Luke 24:27*). He is the cohesive bond that ties and unites both the Old and New Testaments together as a garment is weaved together by an unbreakable fabric. ***"For in Him (Jesus Christ) all things hold together"*** (*Colossians 1:17*).

The following day was Shabbat (Sabbath). That morning after prayer, Robert and I drove into the city of Tiberias to witness to some people as we encountered them on the streets. The Sabbath day in Israel is usually quiet since people are at home resting, leaving many of the stores closed for business. But we felt compelled by the Spirit of God to walk along the promenade next to Lake Galilee (more famously known as "The sea of Galilee" in the Gospels).

As we passed by one store, a man came out of his shop to tell us he was open for business. Tourism has greatly declined in Israel since the Palestinian Intifada occurred three years ago. Israeli retailers are desperate to sell their various items that have been popular with tourists traveling to Israel. The man told us his name was Eli, which in Hebrew means "My God" (see *Psalm 22:1*). Immediately I felt led by God's Spirit to impress on Eli that Messiah has come and is soon to return to Israel. He knew I was talking about Yeshua (Jesus). Robert and I then went on to say that God gave the proof of this claim through the many messianic prophecies contained in the Jewish Bible. Furthermore, we said that God has given the world another sign in Scripture that will indicate that the Messiah's return is soon—that would be the regathering of the Jewish people back into the land God gave to them forever (*Genesis 13:15; 17:7-8*). Thus *Isaiah 11:11-12* is in process of fulfillment in this regard. We further said to Eli that the

Messiah Jesus came to bring us forgiveness, love, joy, peace, and abundant life.

Eli indicated that several other believers in Yeshua, both Jew and Gentile, in Israel and from abroad, came into his shop and also shared the Gospel with him. Robert and I then asked him if he was ready to personally trust in Yeshua as Lord and Messiah. He answered that he was not ready yet. So we then asked him if we could pray for him. He said yes. We prayed that the God of Israel would move on Eli's heart and mind to enable him to be willing to accept Jesus as his Messiah. No doubt when we return to Israel in March, we will water this seed of the Gospel we have planted when we visit Eli again. Pray, dear readers, that Eli will be willing in the day of the Lord's power to trust Jesus as God and Messiah (*Psalm 110:3*).

Eli, who had been witnessed to by other believers in Yeshua, was not quite ready yet to trust in Him. But he did allow Todd and Robert to pray for him.

✝ ✿ ✝ ✿ ✝ ✿ ✝

As our witness to Israel in November of 2003 continued in Tiberias, we stopped at a small grocery store and started talking to the owner, whose name was Yacov (Jacob). We talked about the fact that Bible believers and followers of Yeshua are indebted to the Jewish people for their obedience in being used by God to bring us our Biblical heritage, the Christian faith once delivered unto the saints, and the Messiah through whom all this came about. Upon hearing this, Yacov expressed a genuine interest in the claim the B'rit Hadashah makes that Jesus is the Messiah. This claim is based upon the specific prophecies about the Messiah made in the Tanach centuries before the birth of Jesus.

We offered Yacov the New Testament Scriptures in Hebrew and he took it and opened it to the Gospel of Matthew. When he read the first lines about the genealogy of Jesus, he commented to us that the opening of this Gospel was similar to the book of Genesis — both use the same Hebrew word for "beginning" in the genealogies of Adam (*Genesis 5:11*) and Jesus the Messiah (*Matthew 1:1*). In the former, we have the beginning of the universe and man. In the latter, we have the beginning of the human descent of the Messiah. This astute observation by Yacov was all the more amazing when you consider that, as he admitted to us, he did not regularly read the Jewish Scriptures. But right away he recognized the continuity between the Old Testament and the New Testament. Yacov gratefully accepted the Hebrew

Yacov (left, with his friend and Robert) recognized a similarity and continuity between the Old Testament and the New Testament

New Testament and said he would read it further after having already discovered for himself that it is a Jewish book in concert with the Bible of Judaism.

✝ ✿ ✝ ✿ ✝ ✿ ✝

Our witness in Tel Aviv started slowly, but ended gloriously the first day there. All throughout the afternoon and evening, we stopped at various places and passed out Messianic Jewish Gospel tracts. At every place, there seemed to be a lack of interest and an indifference to our message — some days are like that in this type of ministry to Israel.

Somewhat discouraged, Robert and I decided to head back to the hotel. On our way back, we spotted a young man sitting in a parking attendant booth. We felt especially led by God's Spirit to go over to him and share the Gospel of Yeshua with him. He told us his name was Vladimir. The young man was a Russian Jew that had emigrated from the Ukraine region to Israel. This fact led us to reveal to Vladimir that the prophet Jeremiah predicted that in the last days, immediately before the return of the Messiah, God would gather the Jewish exiles from the far north country (*Jeremiah 16:14-15; 23:7-8*). If one were to look at a map, the one major country directly north of Israel is Russia. Jeremiah predicted that the exodus of Jews from Russia to Israel would exceed in number that of Israel from Egypt. Vladimir's return to Israel, we pointed out to him, was a fulfillment of this prophecy on a smaller scale. The Holy Spirit led us to tell Vladimir that the Messiah came to Israel once before. And right before His return to the Jewish nation, He will restore them back into the land (*Jeremiah 12:14-15*). Many people claiming to be the Messiah have come and gone, we said to him, so how can one know the real Messiah when He comes?

We told Vladimir that God has given us certain marks that would identify the true Messiah when He comes. These marks are found in the many prophecies given in the Jewish Bible. We proceeded to show Vladimir from the Tanach how Yeshua could have been the only one to fulfill them all.

Robert and I went over the plan of salvation with him from the Scriptures and how that the Messiah came the first time to suffer and die so that He could atone for the sins of mankind (we read *Isaiah 53* to him at this point in our witness). He readily acknowledged that he was a sinner and needed God's forgiveness. He understood from Scripture that Yeshua was the prophesied Messiah and why He came — to walk with him and work out the great plan He has for Vladimir's life. When Robert and I asked him if he wanted to receive Yeshua in his life and trust Him for salvation, he said, "absolutely." **Vladimir then prayed with us and asked Yeshua to come into his heart and take control of his life.**

Robert and I were awed and joyful at such a demonstration of such simple, childlike faith. Vladimir is now a child of God, a Jewish believer born anew to begin a new life with the Savior Who died for him and rose again from the dead so that Vladimir could spend the rest of eternity with the very God who created him for Himself. We left Vladimir with discipleship materials and two copies of the Bible in Hebrew and Russian. Later, we e-mailed contacts of places where he could go for fellowship and worship with other believers in Tel Aviv.

*Vladimir, a young Russian Jew from the Ukraine
accepted Yeshua into his heart and life!*

After spending two days in Tel Aviv, we went to Haifa and did some productive street witnessing there. Once in Haifa, we prayed for God's leading as we walked the streets. While walking at the end of a particular street, a young woman approached us to offer us free literature about the medieval occult writings of the Kabala. This encounter afforded an excellent opportunity to share the Gospel with her.

The Kabala, as she accurately said, teaches that God has made Himself known through a secretive process of calculating the numeric value of the Hebrew letters in the words of the Tanach (the Old Testament text). One therefore has to learn the complicated and esoteric method of decoding what God's message is through the Kabala before he can understand Who God is. In other words, God does not plainly make Himself known through His Word so that any honest and inquiring person can know what He says.

Robert and I countered this erroneous claim by suggesting to her that God in fact created us with reasonable minds so that we could understand what He has done for us through the Messiah He sent to Israel and the world. The problem is that sin stands in the way between a holy God and imperfect man. The only way God can be merciful and just is to have someone who can obey His law perfectly and at the same time pay the penalty for Man's transgressions — that Person was Yeshua Who is the God-man that bridges the gap between the God of Israel and us. Yeshua can perfectly do this because He is both human and divine. She listened attentively but could not give us a counter answer of any practical way to resolve the problem of sin and death which confronts every human, God has conquered this problem by the resurrection of Jesus the Messiah.

The fact of the matter is man can never reach God by the irrational mode of mystic contemplation as Kabalistic teaching asserts, but by God reaching down to us when He became a man Himself in Jesus Christ. This alone is what makes Christianity stand head and shoulders above all the other numerous world religions, including the dead-end mystical meanderings of the Kabala. We offered this young Israeli woman the New Testament in the Hebrew language and reading material about evidence for Jesus being the Messiah of Israel. She readily accepted both after our powerful witness to her about the Messiah. She said in closing that she would read the materials we gave her and give serious thought to the claims of Yeshua. Pray her search for the truth will end with finding the One who says, *"I am the way, the truth, and the life. No man comes to the Father, but by Me"* *(John 14:6).*

This young Israeli woman desperately needed to hear the truth after being taken in by the Kabala theory

✝ ✡ ✝ ✡ ✝ ✡ ✝

While in Jaffa, one witnessing encounter found us in a deep discussion with a customer representative at a music store. His name was Aryeh. Both he and his friend with him, we discovered, were moral relativists. They did not believe there are such things as moral absolutes or that truth in general is a certain and fixed element of reality. Yet in their philosophical claim that there are no moral absolutes, they were paradoxically asserting what they claim was not true.

For in saying there are no absolutes, one automatically claims an absolute by saying there are absolutely no absolutes.

In spite of this, Aryeh and his friend failed to see the absurdity of their philosophical position which was contradictory and self-defeating. Robert and I gave an extensive witness demonstrating the reliability and historical accuracy of the Bible by way of the foretold history of Israel from 3,500 years ago with Moses up to the present time. But alas, all of this for the present time seemed to fall on deaf ears. Both of them outright rejected our testimony. Aryeh vociferously exclaimed he did not believe in Yeshua. We countered his unbelief by saying God will answer that unbelief and show Himself true. Yeshua is the Messiah and if Aryeh would ask the Lord to show Him with an honest and open heart, He will. Otherwise the very Word he rejects will judge him on the last day just as Yeshua says it will, whether Jew or Gentile (see *John 12:47-48*).

Despite extensive witnessing, Aryeh refused to believe in Yeshua

✝ ✡ ✝ ✡ ✝ ✡ ✝

The next day in Haifa, we took the subway into downtown Haifa. Once we got there, a middle-aged man called to us from his fruit juice shop. The man's name was Asher. He gave us freshly squeezed orange juice and was grateful to see Americans visiting Israel, which naturally prompted him to ask us why we came to Israel. Robert and I told him that we came to let the Jewish people know the Messiah has already come. As foretold in the Tanach, the Messiah is soon to return. The prophetic sign is the restoration of Jews back to their ancient homeland.

Asher knew that by us saying the Messiah has already come, we were talking about Yeshua from Nazareth. Asher then named other persons in Jewish history who made the same claims about being the Messiah as Jesus did. "So", he asked, "how can one know who the Messiah really is?" "It is true," we replied, "that anyone can claim to be the Messiah. But only one person could truly be the Messiah by virtue of fulfilling certain and specific prophecies about the Messiah found in the Jewish Scriptures." Asher replied that Jewish people in general couldn't accept Jesus as Messiah. We said in return that this rejection was not based on a clear reading and understanding of Scripture, but upon the misleading traditions of the rabbis, cultural upbringing, and the sad fact that many so called "Christians" have persecuted and killed the Jewish people down through the centuries. All of which has engendered and instilled an inherent rejection of Jesus

Asher was grateful to see Americans visiting Israel

being the Messiah. So this misguided belief is not really rooted and based in Scripture since the case for Jesus being the Messiah is directly found in the Jewish Bible. Asher went on to remark that as far as he could remember Isaiah was the first person in the Bible to mention the Messiah. Robert and I told him that it was Job and Moses who were actually the first ones to speak about the coming of Messiah. We then showed Asher in the Hebrew text the Messianic prophecy God gave Moses in *Deuteronomy 18:15*. In this prophecy, Moses predicted to the nation of Israel that the Lord would raise up the preeminent Prophet who would be superior to all the prophets of Israel who came before Him.

This prophecy obviously points to the Messiah, and if one believes in Moses, then by logical deduction one will believe in the prophet Messiah who would be sent by God to Israel. We then showed Asher in Hebrew from the Gospel of John the passage where Jesus affirmed the prophecy of Moses in *Deuteronomy 18*. Asher read what Yeshua said in *John 5:45-47* that if a Jewish person claims to believe in the Torah (the first five books of the Bible written by Moses), he or she will believe in Jesus the Messiah, the One Moses foretold in *Deuteronomy 18:15* would come. If then you reject Jesus' words, you automatically reject the writings of Moses.

After reading these verses from Scripture, Asher's eyes widened with astonishment over the inescapable fact that not to believe in Yeshua as the Messiah is the same thing as not believing Moses either, the very one who gave the legal code for Judaism. The Ruach Hakodesh (Hebrew for Holy Spirit) was convicting Asher. Robert and I offered him a list of many other prophecies made about the Messiah that were graciously given to us by Zola Levitt — our main sponsor of "To the Jew First" ministry that we conduct in Israel.

Asher was visibly challenged and amazed at the words of Jesus and said he would look at the Messianic literature we gave him concerning the One about whom Moses and the prophets had written.

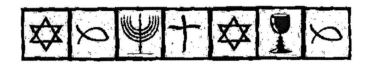

¹⁴ Thus says the LORD: "Against all My evil neighbors who touch the inheritance which I have caused My people Israel to inherit— behold, I will pluck them out of their land and pluck out the house of Judah from among them. ¹⁵ Then it shall be, after I have plucked them out, that I will return and have compassion on them and bring them back, everyone to his heritage and everyone to his land.

Jeremiah 12:14-15

CHAPTER 9:

Comforting the People of God

March 2004 - *Todd's seventh mission trip to Israel, once again accompanied by Robert Cuccia*

March's Gospel 2004 outreach began in Tiberias, Israel. Robert Cuccia and I spent three days here with follow up visits to people we had spoken to in November.

Before we embarked on March's outreach, the Holy Spirit spoke to my heart during my prayer time to go and revisit a young man we witnessed to in Tiberias on our November 2003 Gospel outreach. His name was Eli and he works in a souvenir shop in Tiberias. The Spirit of God pressed upon my mind that when we saw Eli again, we were to strongly urge him to accept Yeshua by faith as his Lord and Savior. As you may recall, in the previous chapter, I wrote that when we witnessed to Eli and shared the Gospel with him, he was not quite ready to accept Yeshua. This time, when we arrived at the shop where he worked, one of his co-workers was there but Eli was not working that day. So he called Eli on the phone and within five minutes, Eli came to the shop to visit with us.

Our visit with him lasted for over two and a half hours. The content of our discussion was to remind him about what

On this visit, Eli was ready to ask Yeshua into his life as his personal Savior

Robert and I discussed with him in November. A key principle in evangelism is after planting a Gospel seed, follow up and water that seed later so in the end, if possible, you can reap a saved soul for Jesus the Messiah.

The central theme of our follow-up witness to Eli this time was the examination of the historic and prophetic proofs for Jesus being the Messiah and the need for salvation by Him. To that end, we informed Eli that man's basic problem is that he has separated himself from God by sin. Sin is the violation of God's law and willful disobedience to His will produces death. No man by his own effort can remove the barrier between God and man that sin creates. Only God can solve the problem of death and separation that sin brought on all humanity.

The sin barrier can only be removed by trust in God's Word and by having the blood of atonement (see *Habakkuk 2:4; Leviticus 17:11*). We further explained to Eli that the blood atonement was first established by God in the Old Testament through the animal sacrifices offered by the Levitical priests in the Tabernacle and the Temple in Jerusalem. But the animal sacrifices provided only a temporary solution for sin. Then God sent Jesus the Messiah to sacrifice Himself on the cross as the permanent and final atonement for the sins of mankind. This perfect sacrifice for sin by the suffering Messiah, we said to Eli, was foretold in *Isaiah 53*. We went over that great prophetic chapter with him. This prophecy, made over 700 years before the birth of Jesus Christ, is one of the many that clearly identifies who the Messiah would be.

Another great Messianic prophecy we showed Eli was the prophecy of *Daniel 9:26* where it was predicted the Messiah would come before the destruction of the second Temple of Jerusalem in A.D. 70. History has verified that only Jesus of Nazareth could have fulfilled these and many other prophecies written in Scripture about the Messiah.

After this lengthy Biblical witness, we said to Eli that God has provided complete forgiveness and new life through the atonement of Yeshua on the cross. All a person has to do is believe and pray to receive Him in one's life as Lord and Savior.

During the course of our extensive Gospel witness to Eli, he was visibly moved and convicted by the greatness of God's love for him. Indeed, several times he put his head down into his hands and his eyes were welling up with tears. **When we invited him to personally ask Christ into his life, he said he was ready. He prayed with us and placed his trust in Yeshua as the Messiah - the One who died for our sins and rose from death to give us eternal life.** Once Eli made this momentous decision, Robert and I encouraged him to attend a Messianic congregation where he could fellowship with other Israeli believers in Yeshua. To that end we put him in contact with a prominent Messianic believer in that area.

✟ ✧ ✟ ✧ ✟ ✧ ✟

Another person we had witnessed to in November was a young Jewish lady named Deborah who worked at a local restaurant in Tiberias. This time, when we went back to this eatery, she was there. When she saw Robert and me, she remembered who we were. As with Eli, we continued our

*Deborah remembered Robert and Todd
from their previous visit*

Gospel witness to her. We made sure to share with Deborah that our profound and abiding love for the Jewish people came from Yeshua the Jewish Messiah Who placed it in our hearts. Deborah amazingly told us that she believed that by looking at our eyes which reflected such love! She said we should come to Israel full-time with such a message.

Please pray as we continue to go and take the Gospel to Israel, that we build lasting friendships with the Jewish people like Deborah. Pray that she will come to see by the Holy Spirit's enlightenment her need for Yeshua in her life and receive Him as Messiah and Savior, even as Eli has already done through this effective ministry.

✝ ✡ ✝ ✡ ✝ ✡ ✝

On our second day of witnessing in Tiberias, Robert Cuccia and I went back to visit a man by the name of Yehudah who owns a fishing supply shop (July 2003's Gospel outreach). He remembered us from the last time we visited him a year ago and wanted to know if we were still doing the same thing in Israel. Robert and I said that we are committed to sharing the good news to the Chosen People about Jesus the Messiah until death.

Yehudah was more open this year and accepted a free Hebrew copy of the B'rit Hadashah

Yehudah seemed more open than he was a year ago when we talked to him the first time about Jesus being the Messiah. Like the last time, Yehudah continued to have questions about the problem of evil and the existence of God. As we patiently answered his questions from the Scriptures, you could visibly see that he was more open to listen about the supernatural reality of Jesus the Messiah.

Last year, he declined to accept a free Hebrew copy of the New Testament. But this time, I felt moved by the Holy Spirit to offer a free copy to him again, and this time he accepted it and said he would read it. Robert and I were encouraged as we left him at how God is slowly opening this man's heart to the Gospel. We shall continue our witness to him when we return, Lord willing, in the fall.

✝ ✿ ✝ ✿ ✝ ✿ ✝

Next, we revisited Katrina at the tourist information center. This time Robert and I witnessed to her and her co-worker, Nara. Katrina believes that the Jews will receive the Messiah, whoever He may be, when He comes, whether He be Yeshua or some other person. We flat out told her that the Messiah has already come to Israel and is coming again when Jesus

Todd gets into an animated discussion with Katrina and her co-worker, Nara

of Nazareth returns. He is the only One who could have fulfilled all the major prophecies made about the Messiah's first coming in the Tanach.

Anyone can claim to be the Messiah and there have risen over forty false messiahs in Jewish history. But not one of them fulfilled those specific messianic prophecies like Jesus obviously did. God spelled out through these prophecies who would be the true Messiah when He comes.

We went through some of these prophecies with Katrina and Nara. Robert told them that if the Jewish people reject the Messiah Jesus, they are liable to accept the false messiah (the Anti-Christ). Indeed, Jesus predicted this very same thing in *John 5:43* when He said to the unbelieving Jews of His day, ***"I have come in My Father's name, and you do not receive Me: if another comes in his own name, him you will receive."***

Of the two, Nara appeared more open to the Gospel truth. I gave her a Gospel tract detailing God's historical program for the Jewish people. I explained how it revolves around the first and second comings of Jesus the Messiah. We also gave her a Hebrew Bible containing the New Testament.

Dear reader, pray that both of these Jewish ladies search and study these Messianic prophecies from the Scriptures to behold and believe that Yeshua is the Messiah.

✝ ✡ ✝ ✡ ✝ ✡ ✝

The next day, we journeyed to Qiryat Shimona—a city near the Israeli and Lebanon border. As we were walking in the business district, Robert and I decided to go into an arts and crafts shop to talk to the owner, Armand. He expressed a calm interest in wanting to read the Scriptures that we offered him, especially the Bible that included a Hebrew New Testament. Amazingly enough, this Jewish man never owned a copy of the Scriptures and was quite eager to accept a copy from us.

We shared with Armand that the portrait that is painted within the sacred pages of Scripture is a picture of the Jewish

Messiah of Israel Who came to redeem man from the power of evil and death. Armand replied that the identity of the Messiah couldn't be known as of yet since He has not come.

Armand was truly interested in reading the Scriptures, a copy of which he had never owned until given one by Todd and Robert

We affirmed that the Bible does in fact provide numerous prophecies about the Messiah and the person who fulfilled them would, by virtue of that fact, be the Messiah! Robert and I explained to him that the only person in history who has done this is Jesus of Nazareth.

To that end we offered historic proof of this to Armand. We gave him a list of the major Messianic prophecies fulfilled by Yeshua and told him to look them up in the copy of the Hebrew Scriptures we gave him. He thanked us. Several minutes later, after we left his shop, I looked back from the end of the street and saw Armand at the entrance of his business reading the Scriptures.

Pray that in doing so the Ruach Hakodesh (Hebrew for the Holy Spirit) will enlighten him to see Messiah Jesus in all the Scripture and lead him to trust Yeshua as Lord and Messiah.

After walking a block or two, Robert and I decided to stop in a department store to look at watches. A sales lady by the name of Natalie asked us if we needed any help. In the course of our conversation with her, we discovered that Natalie was from the Ukraine and immigrated to Israel when she was 14 years old. We told her that the immigration of the two million or so Russian Jews to Israel since the early 1990's was foretold to occur in the last days right before the return of the Messiah to Israel.

We showed the prophecies found in *Jeremiah 16:14-15* and *23:7-8* that predict this very event, adding that her immigration from the former Soviet Union to Israel was by the hand of God a preordained event that was foretold in the Word of God some 2,500 years ago! Robert and I further said to her that God not only wants to restore the Jewish people to their ancient homeland, but most of all desires that they receive Yeshua the Messiah who will eventually return to the land of Israel.

Natalie said her mother was a believer in Yeshua and she knew about Him. We gave her a Gospel tract in Hebrew that shows how one can be saved through faith in Yeshua the

Natalie said her mother is a believer in
Yeshua, so she knows about Him

Messiah. She heartily thanked us and said she would read the Hebrew Scriptures and the Gospel literature we gave her.

✝ ✡ ✝ ✡ ✝ ✡ ✝

After lunch, Robert and I went to an open market place. While walking through there, we stopped by a stand to look at a strange looking instrument for sale. After we inquired as to what it was, the young vendor told us that the instrument was for cutting corns that grow on one's toes. The young vendor selling these things and other eccentric items was a young Jewish man by the name of Valleré. Our curiosity over this strange looking object served as an open door to witness to this young man about having a personal relationship with the God of Israel through His Son Jesus the Messiah.

Valleré told us that his father is Jewish but his mother is a Russian Orthodox Christian. So from this mixed religious background, he had some knowledge of Jesus and Christianity. Robert and I boldly challenged him, with care and concern, about making a personal commitment of his life to Yeshua as Lord and Messiah. He told us in reply that he had been thinking about this very thing for some time but was afraid of the negative reactions he would receive from his Israeli peers if he did make such a commitment of faith.

Valleré admitted to a spiritual connection with Todd and Robert after their discussion about his salvation

Robert and I told him that when we came to trust Christ and follow Him faithfully, we also had faced scorn and rejection from many of our peers and so-called "friends" who were not true friends in the end.

We went on to tell him that God has made Jesus the only one who can deliver us from the power of evil and remove the fear of death by promising us a home in heaven and a resurrection body (*John 14:1-6; 1 Corinthians 15:51-58*). At the conclusion of our effective witness to him, Valleré expressed that our deep, spiritual discussion with him established a spiritual connection between him and us.

Dear readers, pray that Valleré's fear of man will be replaced with a bold faith in the God of Israel and His Son Jesus the Messiah. We left him with a Gospel tract showing from the Scriptures how one can be saved by trusting in Christ. Lord willing, we will follow up on Valleré when we return to Israel in the near future.

✝ ✧ ✝ ✧ ✝ ✧ ✝

After we left Tiberias, Robert and I drove to Jerusalem. As we left the hotel to go and pick up some more Hebrew New Testaments, Robert and I stopped to witness to the security guard just outside the hotel. Her name was Marina. She had emigrated from Russia to Israel four years ago. Upon learning this about her life, Robert and I explained to her that God had foretold through the prophet Jeremiah that He would bring the Jewish people back from the far north country of Russia to the land of Israel (*Jeremiah 16 and 23*). Marina said in response to this that she was an atheist. But you could tell that she was not very firm in this conviction.

I gave her my testimony of how I was a strong and militant atheist before Yeshua the Messiah revealed Himself to me when I was desperately searching for the truth to the meaning of life. Robert and I further said to Marina that if she really wants to know the truth about God and His Son Jesus the Messiah all she has to do is seek Him with an honest and open heart and He will convincingly reveal Himself to her.

For the Lord promises in *Jeremiah 33:3* to all honest inquirers, ***"Call to Me, and I will answer you, and show you great and mighty things, which you do not know."***

Marina, a security guard at this hotel, claimed to be an atheist, but she accepted and read the literature given her

The next day, we graciously resumed our witness with Marina. She said that she read the Jewish Gospel literature we gave her. The nature of this follow up witness focused on the miracle of the Incarnation and how the God of Israel desires to have a personal relationship with her by becoming a flesh and blood human being so that He could reach out to her in the person of Yeshua the Messiah.

After we concluded our witness with Marina, we went to pray and share the Messiah at the Western Wall.

✝ ✿ ✝ ✿ ✝ ✿ ✝

After we left the Western Wall, Robert and I stopped at a restaurant to buy lunch. Two young men came in after us and both were Armenians who lived in the Armenian quarter of the old city of Jerusalem. We began to speak to one of the men. His name was Puray.

When he discovered we were messengers of the Gospel of Jesus Christ, Puray candidly admitted to us that he was struggling with a drinking problem. We discussed with him about how our own past, many years ago, was riddled with drugs and alcohol. Robert and I were both enslaved by them until the Lord Jesus permanently liberated us from such bondage. I personally told Puray that such a profligate lifestyle nearly destroyed me before I reached the age of 20. We told Puray that the only real and effective answer that can free him from the bondage of addiction is the Messiah who came to set the captives free (*Luke 4:18*).

I told him my liberation and restored dignity from the ravages of drug addiction came when the Lord Jesus unexpectedly manifested His visible glory to me which forever changed my life for the exceeding good. Puray asked why God did not show him a sign like that. My response was that God does show signs to each of us in different ways—both subtle and obvious, but we must have eyes to correctly see them as such. Indeed I reminded him that God had spared his life when he foolishly did things that put him in danger of injury or death as a sign of His intervening mercy. Puray readily agreed that this was the case several times in his life.

Robert and I went on to share with Puray that every person needs a spiritual rebirth to change, transform, and liberate a

Robert and Todd spoke to Puray and his friend about spiritual rebirth

person from a life of bondage and sin to the freedom of abundant life in Jesus Christ. Puray said he saw the need for this in his life but was not quite ready to make such a surrender until he bettered himself first.

Robert and I were quick to reply that we are all sinners and must come to God dirty as we are so that He can clean us up. Indeed He invites everyone in the welcoming words of *Isaiah 1:18* to **"Come now, and let us reason together, says the Lord. Though your sins are like scarlet, they shall be white as snow; though they are red like crimson, they shall be white as wool."**

We left Puray a ministry newsletter and instructed him from the Gospel of *John* chapter 3 about the necessity of the spiritual rebirth through faith in the atoning Messiah. Puray was encouraged by our personal testimony of how Jesus Christ changed our lives from an ignoble condition to a noble calling.

Pray for this young man that he will come to the end of himself and see the bankruptcy of alcoholism and turn to the Savior to find true, permanent freedom and new life.

✝ ✿ ✝ ✿ ✝ ✿ ✝

Not more than twenty minutes after we finished our witness with Puray, Robert and I were walking down the street; two young Jewish girls were walking a few feet behind us. I overheard them talking about Mel Gibson's movie *The Passion of the Christ.* I couldn't help but turn back and say to them they needed to go and see this movie. It is a deeply moving depiction of the death of the Jewish Messiah for the sins of mankind. This Suffering Servant of *Isaiah 53* came to redeem the Jewish people. I further reassured the two girls that this masterpiece of a movie is in no way anti-Semitic, having seen the movie twice myself. I further told them that the death of the Messiah for our sins is how the God of Israel has shown His supreme love for the world. I offered both of them a Gospel tract going into further detail about these things. The girls gladly accepted it, thanked us, and wished us a happy Sabbath.

✝ ✡ ✝ ✡ ✝ ✡ ✝

After that, Robert and I sat and rested on a bench. While there, the Holy Spirit spoke to my heart that we were to go by a certain hotel on the way back to where we were staying and witness to the security guard. I initially kept this impression to myself. When we drew near that very hotel with the female security guard in sight, Robert suddenly looked over in that direction and expressed a desire to go over there and talk to that person, saying in effect that we would "have a captive audience." Once again, God confirmed to me by Robert's mutual wish that the Holy Spirit was leading both of us in witnessing about the Messiah to this particular individual.

Her name was Inbal. She had been an intelligence officer with the IDF (Israeli Defense Forces). We said that we are disciples of Yeshua the Jewish Messiah and that God's Word says we are to take His message of salvation first to the Jewish people (*Romans 1:16*). For it was to them the Messiah would first come and He did so some 2,000 years ago. Robert and I further exclaimed to Inbal that the God of Abraham, Isaac, and Jacob wants to have a personal relationship with her, so much so that He became a Jewish man born in the

Inbal, another hotel security guard, accepted a copy of the Jewish Scriptures, including the New Testament

land of Israel to reach out and take hold of her. This was not a Gentile invention but was foretold to occur through the Jewish people who wrote the Scriptures of which the central character is the Messiah.

When asked by us if she read the Jewish Scriptures, Inbal said she had read the Tanach but not the Jewish New Testament. We asked her if she would like a free copy of the Jewish Scriptures that included the New Testament because it completes the revelation of God to man as found in the Messiah. She answered "yes" and accepted a copy of both the Old and New Testaments in the Hebrew language.

✝ ✡ ✝ ✡ ✝ ✡ ✝

When we returned to our hotel, we were also able to witness to a young lady whose name was Yehudit (Judith in English). After talking with her for a bit, we discovered that her world-view was basically one of a secular humanist. In her view, man was nothing more than a highly evolved animal that emerged from nothing and goes into death to become nothing again! We reflected back to her that the true description of man, according to her philosophical construct, is that he lives in futility and merely lives to die.

The atheistic existentialist philosopher Jean Paul Sartre basically came to this hopeless conclusion as well. Yehudit had to admit that carried to its logical end her worldview resulted in a hopeless and meaningless condition. We explained to her about the true fact that God made man in His own image (*Genesis 1:26-27*) first as a spiritual being indwelling a physical body and placed him in a perfect environment to enjoy Holy fellowship and felicity with the Creator. But man chose against this, preferring his self will above the divine will and pursued a path of rebellion and disobedience to God bringing death, evil, and decay upon himself and all human posterity (*Genesis 3*). This problem is called sin and has separated man from God.

But God has not left us under the domain and power of sin and death. He has sent us a Redeemer and Mediator to perfectly represent God to man and who can also be a true representative of man to God—that person or mediator would of logical necessity have to be both divine and human—the God-man. This person is what the Bible calls the Messiah and all the prophecies about Him are uniquely and exclusively fulfilled in Jesus of Nazareth. He alone is the true Messiah of Israel that reconciles man with God through His atoning sacrifice. The story of the Bible is one of redemption about God's infinite love for Man culminating in giving His one and only unique Son for us.

Yehudit took a Messianic Gospel tract from us and said she would read it. She really did not now how to respond to what we told her, probably because it was the first time she heard the good news of Jesus the Messiah. Pray that upon further reflection the Spirit of God will lead her to place her trust in Jesus as Lord and Savior.

✝ ✿ ✝ ✿ ✝ ✿ ✝

Later in the evening while walking in Jerusalem, we stopped at an intersection and happened to notice a Jewish young man carrying a backpack walking towards us. Both Robert and I felt compelled to talk with him about Yeshua

Elnatahn, studying to become a Rabbi, was given proof of Who the true Messiah is

being the Messiah. The young man's name was Elnatahn. He told us he was attending a Yeshiva school studying to be a Rabbi. After expressing our gratitude for what the Jewish people gave the world via the Bible, the Messiah, and the Christian faith, our conversation with him shifted to the identity of the Messiah and how one could know Him when He comes to Israel. Elnatahn said that only through the Rabbis and years of study could one possible determine who the Messiah would be. In other words, like so many in the rabbinic community of Judaism, one must look to the opinions of the rabbis to answer this all-important question. But the problem with that, as we pointed out to him, is that the rabbis have so often contradicted themselves and the Scripture when trying to answer who the Messiah would be when he comes.

The only foolproof method whereby we can ascertain the identity of the Messiah is by looking at the Holy Scriptures themselves where many detailed prophecies about Messiah's life are found. Robert and I mentioned several Messianic prophecies to this young man like:

- ✡ **the Messiah would descend from David's family line (*Jeremiah 23:5-6*);**
- ✡ **He would be born in Bethlehem (*Micah 5:2*);**
- ✡ **He would rise from the dead (*Psalm 16:10*); and**
- ✡ **Messiah would die as an innocent sacrifice for the sins of Israel and the world (*Isaiah 53*).**

Indeed, when we showed Elnathan the prophecy of the suffering Messiah in *Isaiah 53* without suggesting who the prophet was talking about, he exclaimed from reading the text himself that the passage was talking about the Messiah! It was that obvious.

Concerning the prophecy of *Isaiah 53*, we explained to Elnathan that this was the sole purpose for the first coming of the Messiah—to suffer and die for the salvation of mankind. We informed Elnathan that all these prophecies have been fulfilled in the birth, life, death, and resurrection of Yeshua of Nazareth. We left him some reading materials about why Jesus is the Messiah of Israel. He thanked us and left. Robert and I prayed right after he left that the God of Israel would illuminate his heart and mind that Yeshua is the Messiah and worthy of total trust and commitment.

✞ ✿ ✞ ✿ ✞ ✿ ✞

The next day after morning prayer, Robert and I decided to do some witnessing for Messiah on Ben Yehudah Street. On our way there, we stopped at the Great Synagogue of Jerusalem. There, we briefly talked to the security guard at the front door. We talked to him about the greatest Jew who ever lived and is alive today—Jesus the Messiah. We gave him a Gospel tract that provides a historical overview of the history of the Jewish people from the exodus to the second coming of the Messiah back to Israel.

✞ ✿ ✞ ✿ ✞ ✿ ✞

Once we arrived on Ben Yehudah Street, Robert and I went into a gift shop that was owned and operated by an elderly man named Yo'el (Joel in English). We said to him that we came to Israel to bless the Jewish people with the greatest blessing God brought to the world through the Chosen People. He inquired what that was. We replied that it

Yo'el (Joel) accepted the free copy of the B'rit Hadashah

was the Messiah whose coming was foretold in the Jewish Scriptures in several particulars with amazing detail and foresight. The Messianic prophecies were given by God so that when the Messiah did come there would be no doubt as to His identity by virtue of the fact He would fulfill the prophecies foretold about Him.

As Joel listened, we boldly proclaimed to him that Israel's Messiah already came and fulfilled those prophecies that pertained to His first coming and will fulfill the rest that remain when He returns. History has proven this person is identified to be none other than Yeshua of Nazareth as documented by personal eyewitnesses in the B'rit Hadashah (the New Testament). But those in Israel must read and study this very Jewish book to know that. We then offered Joel a free copy of the B'rit Hadashah and he graciously accepted it.

✝ ✡ ✝ ✡ ✝ ✡ ✝

Continuing our Gospel witness on Ben Yehudah Street in Jerusalem, we revisited a jewelry store where I had previously bought a silver Mezuzah. The owner of the shop was a man

Danny listened as Robert and Todd explained how the present regathering of the Jewish people back to their land was predicted in the Bible

by the name of Danny. Robert and I shared with him how the land of Israel is unlike any other land in the world for the simple fact it is the only piece of land God set apart to give a people, the Jewish people for an *"everlasting possession"* (*Genesis 17:7-8*). The purpose for this was to choose a place and a people so that God could bring redemption to the whole world through the Jewish Savior.

We then said to Danny that the present regathering of the Jewish people back into the land of Israel was the very thing predicted in the Scriptures to occur before this Messiah returns. He listened with notable interest; as well he should since such startling but ancient news predicted long ago directly concerns him and his people.

But a person does not have to wait for His return to receive the Messiah. You can look at the evidence for Yeshua being the Messiah of Israel as foretold in the Tanach and fulfilled in the B'rit Hadashah and accept Him now into your life.

After pondering on this for a little bit, Danny thanked us and we gave him a Gospel tract showing the evidence for Jesus being the Messiah of Israel and how a Jewish person can accept Him now and be saved.

✝ ✡ ✝ ✡ ✝ ✡ ✝

After lunch, Robert spotted a guitar store, and being an amateur guitarist, he naturally felt drawn to the store. This personal interest of his proved to be an opportunity to share the good news of the Jewish Messiah.

After Robert briefly looked at the guitars, we told the manager of the store, Doron, that we were sent by a prominent Messianic ministry (Zola Levitt) and congregation (Shalom, Shalom). These ministries seek to educate Gentile Christians in America about the Jewish roots of their faith and educate Jewish people in Israel about the Messiahship of Yeshua and the Jewish authorship of the New Testament. To underscore the latter, we gave Doron and his co-worker Messianic Gospel tracts and literature to read.

A seed was planted at this guitar shop hopefully in the hearts of both Doron and his co-worker

✝ ✿ ✝ ✿ ✝ ✿ ✝

The Lord then led us to a cigar store to talk to the owner, Eli. He was a hard and skeptical person given to sarcasm, which is not an unusual attitude for the modern secular Israeli. I mentioned that the Bible predicted that the restoration of the Jewish people to their ancient homeland after a long worldwide dispersion would signal the soon return of the Messiah. Eli excitedly, but skeptically replied, "When will He return, and how many more innocent citizens of Israel will be victims of terrorism?" We certainly sympathized with him and listened with concern and compassion.

Eli went on to say he had friends die in some of the terrorist attacks. Robert and I expressed that the perennial hatred for the Jewish people is really satanic in origin because the adversary (the devil) hates and seeks to destroy the objects of God's love. For God chose the Jewish people as a messianic people through whom the Messiah would come to destroy the devil's supernatural grip and hold on mankind (*1 John 3:8*). The current volatile situation of Israel in the world, which will eventually lead all the nations to mount an assault against this tiny land, will result in the Battle of Armageddon and the return of the Messiah to save Israel from annihilation. This is now beginning to emerge with the global community's hatred (the UN, the EU, etc.,) and rising opposition to the only real democracy in the Middle East.

Sometimes the best ministry to those in Israel who have suffered the violence of terrorism is to listen and comfort them without saying a word, letting them vent, so to speak. And by those caring qualities, they know that the Yeshua we proclaim is a Messiah who loves His people and puts that love in those who truly follow Him.

✝ ✡ ✝ ✡ ✝ ✡ ✝

One memorable witnessing encounter on our March 2004 Gospel outreach to Israel occurred in the Jewish Quarter of the Old City in Jerusalem. It took place in a section called the *Cardo*. The word *Cardo* is a Latin word that means, "heart." Thus, the *Cardo* portion of any city in the Roman Empire was the heart of the city, the main thoroughfare where commercial activity took place. In Jesus' day the *Cardo* formed the central part of Jerusalem and was the busiest part of the city. Indeed, when one walks through the ancient ruins of that time, he or she is

Udi Merioz, owner of The Blue and White Art Gallery and famous Israeli painter, visits all the Holy sites visited by Yeshua

literally walking on the same marble stones Jesus and his twelve disciples walked on.

In the *Cardo,* the tourist or shopping resident of Jerusalem is greeted with modern shops and museums of various sorts. Robert Cuccia and I had heard about a famous art gallery in this area called The Blue and White Art Gallery owned by famous Israeli painter Udi Merioz. Udi has been the official art curator for the last four Prime Ministers of Israel.

Once we arrived, Udi took us on a tour of his gallery. His paintings are scenes and holy sites of Jerusalem like the Western Wall, the Temple Mount, and the various gates of the Holy City. On our tour, Udi showed us one of his paintings not customarily found in an art gallery of an Observant (Orthodox) Jew—the Church of the Holy Sepulcher in Jerusalem where Christian tradition claims the tomb of Jesus was located. Viewing this painting done by Udi was the door the Ruach HaKodesh (Hebrew for "Holy Spirit") was opening before us to share the Gospel of Yeshua the Messiah of Israel with one of his own Jewish countrymen.

I asked Udi, point blank, why he felt led to paint a holy site that has enormous implications not only for Christians but for the whole human race. He struggled to give a definite answer, as if he were coming to terms with the life of the greatest Jew who ever lived. Udi said that, unlike most Jewish people in Jerusalem, he made it a point to take his family to every holy site in Jerusalem where Yeshua visited, taught, died, and rose again. His reason for painting one of the reputed locations for the burial and resurrection of Yeshua was that it had a certain aura of spiritual light and attraction for him. Udi did not fully realize the cosmic significance of this location and what transpired there almost two thousand years ago until I informed him.

While I was talking with Udi, Robert was busy sharing with Udi's father (who sadly passed away a month after Robert and I visited them). He shared about the major thread of continuity that runs through the Tanach (Old Testament) and B'rit Hadashah (New Testament) joining them as one,

Robert and Todd had a great witnessing experience with Udi and his father

which is the Person, program, and prophecies of the Messiah. The compelling evidence from Scripture, ancient Jewish history, and fulfilled prophecy indubitably points to Jesus of Nazareth being the Messiah of Israel.

Meanwhile, I said to Udi that the resurrection of Jesus the Messiah declared by the early Jewish church and depicted in his painting is the most significant act of the God of Israel that occurred in the city of Jerusalem among the Jewish people. It is, in fact, of maximum benefit to every human being for all time (I briefly elaborated on *1 Corinthians 15* here). For in this grandest of miracles, the scourge and reign of death has met its end.

The next painting Udi showed me was both spiritually revealing to me as a Bible-believing Christian and to Udi as an Observant Orthodox Jewish person. His painting had the Western Wall (the most holy site in all of Judaism) in the background and in front lying on a table covered by a white tablecloth was a Tallit (a Jewish prayer shawl worn by adult Jewish men) and a Shofar (a ram's horn). Udi explained to me what the painting meant. The Tallit is worn for two reasons in Judaism; one, for a time of prayer and communion with God in daily life, and two, it is worn in death when a Jewish man is buried. Udi said the Shofar was symbolic for when God calls us up from the grave at the resurrection.

Immediately I saw in this painting from the perspective of the New Testament the great doctrine of the Rapture portrayed here, which teaches that the Messiah Jesus will return, and with a great blast of the heavenly Shofar (trumpet), the dead in Messiah will be resurrected from death first and then we which are alive shall be transformed from mortal to immortal and be caught up together to meet the Lord Jesus in the air (see *1 Thessalonians 4:14-18; 1 Corinthians 15:51-58*). When I shared this New Testament teaching with Udi he was quite intrigued and said that he could see that meaning in his picture as well!

Both Robert and I ended up purchasing two beautiful paintings by this renowned, humble, and gentle artist whose father and he opened their hearts to the message about the Messiah of Israel. As a free gift, they gave us a book of old engravings and illustrations of Jerusalem. In return we offered them a Hebrew New Testament to learn more about why Yeshua is the Savior of the Jewish people and the world.

✟ ✪ ✟ ✪ ✟ ✪ ✟

While we were heading back to our hotel from the art gallery, another profitable witnessing encounter in Jerusalem happened when Robert and I stopped into an art shop were Judaic art was custom made from silver and gold hand assembled by expert designers. One of the head designers greeted us. She was a Jewish woman named Gracia who originally came from Morocco. She showed Robert and me many of the fine artwork handcrafted at the shop. After this presentation, we got into an in-depth conversation with Gracia about the Jewish roots of biblical Christianity. Naturally, our discussion in her office focused on who Jesus of Nazareth was. The amazing thing in this Gospel witness to this woman was that she took an hour and a half out of her busy schedule to personally discuss the Gospel message and the divine claims Yeshua made for Himself. Our witness to her covered several areas that included how the Feasts of Israel, particularly Passover, point to the life, death, and resurrection of Jesus the Messiah.

Gracia's response was that God is known by many names and all religions lead to Him in the end. Robert and I respectfully disagreed by pointing out that her pluralistic assertion was simply not true for the simple fact that each particular world religion when compared with one another are mutually exclusive and what superficial similarities exist between them are greatly eclipsed by their irreducible differences.

For example, Hinduism, which is a polytheistic belief system, affirms the existence of millions of different gods while Christianity, Judaism, and Islam affirm the monotheistic belief that there is only one God. Even these three worldviews differ on defining Who that one God is. We further commented that the Bible could be trusted above all other religious books because it has the stamp of a proven track record of accurately predicting the future with amazing specificity one-hundred percent of the time.

Her reply to this reflected the typical view expressed by people with a relativistic and subjective view of truth—that what we said about Yeshua and the veracity of Scripture is true only because we believe it to be true. Robert and I correctly pointed out that truth wherever found in history, the physical world, or in the spiritual realm is not validated by a person's belief (it maybe confirmed here) but is true by the very nature of the case or object itself. There is such a thing as objective truth not only in the physical realm with the law of physics but also in the spiritual and theological dimensions as well with regard to the Person and nature of God.

We used the example that one can sincerely believe that a tree in his yard is the all-powerful God, yet that very tree cannot create out of nothing or possess the power to perform a miracle such as a resurrection from the dead as the God of Israel did when raising Jesus of Nazareth from the dead almost two-thousand years ago in the city of Jerusalem.

*Gracia took an hour and a half out of her
busy day to talk about the Gospel*

Gracia thanked us and mentioned the fact that there were other Jewish believers in Israel that had also shared the faith of Jesus the Messiah with her. The Lord, apparently, sent Robert and me to water this Gospel seed that had previously been planted by our Jewish brethren in Israel so that eventually she might be saved (*John 4:37-38*). The Holy Spirit is obviously dealing with Gracia in the attempt to bring her to faith in Yeshua as Lord and Messiah. She could not accept Jesus being the eternal God revealed in flesh at that point in time because of belief that all religions are equally valid. But when we pointed out to her that her own Jewish prophets foretold the Messiah would in fact be divine she replied she did not know that (see *Isaiah 9:6; Micah 5:1-2*).

Our prayer is that she will read and study from the Hebrew New Testament and the Jewish Gospel tracts we gave her. Pray that she comes to the knowledge of the truth that she may know the one and only true God of Israel and Yeshua the Messiah (*John 17:3*).

✞ ✡ ✞ ✡ ✞ ✡ ✞

Robert and I decided to visit the historic Israel Museum, a museum in Jerusalem near the Knesset, whose chief emphasis is on the material culture and history (past, present, and future) of the land of Israel and the Jewish people. When we arrived at the entrance Robert and I were immediately stopped by a security guard and an elderly man. Both of them informed us that the museum was temporarily closed because someone had left a bag unattended. The bomb squad from the police department came and removed it and the bag later proved harmless.

As we were waiting outside during this process, an elderly man (his name was Avraham) approached us and cordially asked us where we were from. We told him we came from Dallas, Texas. From then on, our conversation focused on the precarious position of Israel being surrounded as a tiny democratic island by a sea of Arab Islamic dictatorships that want nothing less than the destruction of the Jewish State. Robert and I further added that Israel should be allowed to freely pursue, prosecute, and eliminate all terrorists and their organizations for crimes committed against the Jewish State just as America did in Afghanistan and Iraq. Both situations of Israel and America fighting terrorism are the same; and to

Avraham recognized the love of Christ in Todd and Robert just from their verbalized support of Israel

expect Israel to allow an arch-terrorist like Arafat (who was alive at the time of this writing) and his numerous terrorists entities to continue in the name of restraint as requested by the United States government, the E.U., and the United Nations is to hypocritically employ a double standard toward Israel. Israel's hands are still tied by pressure from the global community when it comes to destroying the sinister forces of terrorism within her own borders.

Avraham strongly agreed with our assessment and then proclaimed with happiness in his voice, "I know who you are. You are born-again believers." Obviously, Avraham had some positive contact with Bible believing Christians who love Israel and he was glad to meet some more such as us. We affirmed he was quite correct about us being believers in Jesus. Avraham was very pleased to learn this, which further allowed Robert and me to launch into a discussion about why Yeshua is the Jewish Messiah of Israel.

The primary evidence for this, of course, comes from the many Messianic prophecies found in the Jewish Scriptures. We showed Avraham some of these very prophecies. Once Avraham saw some of these prophecies, he further told us that he was already aware of a few of them. He recalled to Robert and myself his specific knowledge about the prophecy that Messiah will return to the Mount of Olives and go through the Eastern Gate (see *Zechariah 14:4; Ezekiel 43:1-4*). Avraham then surprisingly revealed to us that he was vaguely aware that Jesus of Nazareth could be the Person to fulfill such prophecy, especially since He was pierced in crucifixion and that Israel will see the return of the pierced Messiah as *Zechariah 12:10* foretold when He touches his feet on Olivet at His return.

At this point, Robert and I excitedly related to this eager and open man, whom the Holy Spirit was convicting and enlightening via our Messianic witness, that Yeshua historically fulfilled those prophecies about the Messiah that pertain to the First Coming—to suffer and die to make the final atonement for the sins of mankind. The Scriptures further declare that Yeshua will return to Israel after the Jews are regathered and restored to their homeland. This will fulfill the prophecies that predict the Messiah will return to establish His perfect and righteous kingdom over all the earth from Jerusalem. This Kingdom reign will begin when His feet touch the Mount of Olives.

But a Jewish person does not have to wait until the Messiah returns after the catastrophic twenty-one judgments of the Apocalypse have fallen on the earth leaving one half of mankind destroyed (see *Revelation 6-19*). We concluded our witness to Avraham by saying that Messiah Jesus will enter into the life of any who will simply believe He is the One who died for us and rose again from the dead. He brings us life from death, pardon from God, and a glorious home in heaven.

Avraham was not ready to give his life to the Lord Jesus at that point but he did let us give him a Jewish Gospel tract that shows how an individual can enter into a personal relationship with the God of Israel through the Messiah Jesus through faith, commitment and trust in Him. Pray that this dear man will say yes and receive the Messiah into his heart.

✝ ✧ ✝ ✧ ✝ ✧ ✝

Once we entered the museum, Robert stepped into an office located in one of the galleries. He called me in to help explain to a Jewish lady about how the Feasts of Israel outlined in *Leviticus 23* typify and serve as prophetic truths about the nature of the two comings of the Messiah. Initially, this elderly lady (Maria) was visibly reluctant to receive our testimony. But once she listened to the facts about Jesus being Jewish, the first Christians being Jews, and the New Testament as a Jewish book written by Jewish believers, Maria was somewhat open to the possibility that Jesus could be the Messiah of Israel.

We talked with her for about twenty minutes and she was receptive enough to receive reading material about how Israel's history (past, present, and future) is centered on the first and second advents of Yeshua Hamashiach and how a Jewish person can receive Him for salvation.

✝ ✿ ✝ ✿ ✝ ✿ ✝

The next day in Jerusalem, we hit the streets early in the morning. Robert and I decided to stop in a CD music shop simply called "The Music Store." There, we were able to witness to the store manager. His name was Aiden. He was an agnostic (one who is uncertain about the existence of God). Agnosticism is a self-refuting worldview that claims you cannot be reasonably certain about the existence of God, yet, paradoxically, this view is certain about its uncertainty.

Robert and I told Aiden that the Bible has a proven track record of predicting the future clearly and accurately many times over. A prime example that we gave was the history of Israel (we alluded to *Deuteronomy 28-30* which gives the whole panorama of Israel's national history up to the second coming of Messiah). The scriptures also include the modern day rebirth of Israel in one day (see *Ezekiel 36; Isaiah 66:7-9*)!

Indeed, after studying such numerous and detailed prophecies foretelling Israel's history, the honest mind and discerning eye must conclude that man could not, by his own cognitive powers, accurately predict such events with amazing precision and accuracy based on "luck", "coincidence", or good guessing. The origin for such predictive powers solely comes from an omniscient God who knows the end from the beginning and ancient things before they yet occur, and thus He declared: ***"Remember things that happened at the beginning, long ago—that I am God, and there is no other; I am God and there is none like Me. At the beginning I announce the end, proclaim in advance things not yet done; and say that My plan will hold, I will do everything I please to do... I announced things that happened at the beginning, long ago; they issued from My mouth, I proclaimed them. Then suddenly I acted, and they occurred"*** (*Isaiah 46:9-10; 48:3-5*, quotation from *The Complete Jewish Bible*).

The Lord says from these passages that fulfilled prophecy in the case of Israel's history, foretold in advance and fulfilled in the course of time, proves that the God of Israel exists alone as the only true God. We then shared with Aiden that another major area of Bible prophecy found in Scripture is Messianic prophecy. Robert and I related to Aiden that these prophecies were about the coming Jewish Messiah who redeems man from the power of evil, sin, death, and the devil. But to study these prophecies closely and to know Who they point to, a person has to read them in the Tanach (the Old Testament Scriptures) and compare them with the life and ministry of Yeshua in the B'rit Hadashah (New Testament Scriptures), which shows how they have been fulfilled in Him.

On that note Robert and I gave Aiden a copy of the Old and New Testament Scriptures in Hebrew so that he could study these Messianic prophecies for himself. He accepted them with genuine appreciation.

✝ ✿ ✝ ✿ ✝ ✿ ✝

Later in the day we walked into a New Age bookshop. The Eastern religions and New Age beliefs have quite a widespread appeal in Israel among the young people. At the bookshop, Robert felt the leading of the Holy Spirit to witness to a young Israeli man named Toma (Thomas in Hebrew). Robert was again witnessing to an agnostic. He used simple logic to show Thomas that if God exists He must be perfect by definition. Compared to this notion of perfection man falls short and fights against the imperfection of evil. This evil is called sin.

The problem of sin separates us from a perfect God. If God, being by nature morally perfect, and we are not, the huge difference and disparity of this has created a chasm that cannot be bridged by our own tainted efforts. This is why God must bridge that gap through the Messiah who can be both perfect (divine) and human so that He can reach out to save us from the plight of evil. Unfortunately, Thomas refused the Gospel message, but a seed was planted and we pray

Toma (Thomas) claims to be agnostic and did not accept the Gospel message offered

the Lord will water it that it may blossom into saving faith in Yeshua the Messiah.

✝ ✡ ✝ ✡ ✝ ✡ ✝

Our next witnessing encounter of the day occurred in a sunglasses shop. There we shared Yeshua with three women—Miriam, Mia, and Olga. Robert and I spoke to them about God's covenant faithfulness with the people of Israel that started with the eternal land grant God gave to Abraham and the Jewish people forever (*Genesis 13:15; 17:7-8*).

The remainder of our witness to them focused on the final covenant God made with Israel guaranteeing redemption, the forgiveness of all sin, and eternal life through the Jewish Messiah God sent to Israel. This covenant was promised to the Jewish nation and ratified in the Person of Yeshua the Messiah of Whom Moses and all the prophets point to in the Tanach. The three women knew right away that what we said about Yeshua being the Messiah was solely based on the Jewish Scriptures about historical events that occurred in the land of Israel. To many Jewish people "Jesus" is the pagan god of the Gentiles and the New Testament is a foreign book removed from its Jewish foundations.

Two of the three women (Miriam, Mia, and Olga) witnessed to and grateful for Robert and Todd's support of Israel

The ladies were very grateful that Robert and I came to Israel to encourage the Jewish people and let them know God will not abandon them (*Psalm 121*). We concluded our witness with them by showing them evidence from the Old Testament prophecies about the Messiah's first coming that were clearly fulfilled in the life of Jesus of Nazareth. We gave them several Messianic Gospel tracts providing more evidence for the Messiahship of Jesus and how believing in Him can save a Jewish person.

✟ ✡ ✟ ✡ ✟ ✡ ✟

Later, Robert and I stopped to visit an art gallery. The owner of the gallery was a Jewish woman from France that immigrated to Israel some twenty years ago. When we began to share with her how belief in Yeshua as the Messiah was based upon the Torah and the Prophets, she was resistant to such truth—preferring, as she said, to believe what her rabbis taught about such things. The rabbis erroneously teach their people that belief in Yeshua and the writings of the New Testament are non-Jewish, and therefore not for the Jews.

To disprove this unscriptural and wrong-headed misconception, Robert and I conducted a brief Bible study with her showing her from the Jewish Bible (Old Testament) the major prophecies about the Messiah and how Yeshua fulfilled them in His life from the New Testament. This was simply done to drive home the point that the rabbis are obviously wrong and that both Yeshua and the New Testament are Jewish realities of Israel and therefore were chiefly intended for the Jews.

She rejected reading or accepting the New Testament in Hebrew since the rabbis also prohibit their faithful from owning, let alone reading, a copy of it. She informed us that those who do own it are instructed to burn it. Robert and I stated that to burn a book is censorship. We also said refusing to read the most important book ever written and believing in the central figure of that book (i.e., the Messiah of Israel) also amounts to censorship of the soul that endangers the eternal welfare of the person. On a positive note, we were able to leave her reading materials arguing the case for Jesus being the Messiah and how a Jewish person can come to faith in Him.

²⁴ For I will take you from among the nations, gather you out of all countries, and bring you into your own land. ²⁵ Then I will sprinkle clean water on you, and you shall be clean; I will cleanse you from all your filthiness and from all your idols. ²⁶ I will give you a new heart and put a new spirit within you; I will take the heart of stone out of your flesh and give you a heart of flesh. ²⁷ I will put My Spirit within you and cause you to walk in My statutes, and you will keep My judgments and do them. ²⁸ Then you shall dwell in the land that I gave to your fathers; you shall be My people, and I will be your God.

Ezekiel 36:24-28

CHAPTER 10:

Ambassadors of Messiah

March 2005 - *Todd's eighth evangelistic outreach to Israel, with longtime friend Paul Colley*

Paul Colley, a personal friend, missionary, and co-laborer in Christ for twenty-one years, accompanied me on this outreach. Once Paul and I boarded our flight in New York bound for Tel Aviv, Israel, we immediately felt led by the Holy Spirit to pray that any Jewish person sitting next to us on the flight would be especially open to a witness about Yeshua being the Messiah of Israel.

Not long after that prayer was said, two men sat next to us. One man was named Joseph. He sat next to Paul on the long flight to Israel. He was a middle-aged man with an Orthodox background. He was very genial, tolerant, and open to our bearing testimony about Yeshua being the Jewish Messiah. He asked us about our reasons for traveling to Israel. Paul and I told him that we were sent by several ministries (Zola Levitt, B'rit Hadashah, and Shalom, Shalom Messianic congregation) who support Israel and send us there to spread the good news of Yeshua the Messiah's first coming and His soon return to the land of Israel as King of kings and Lord of lords.

The man sitting next to me was a cordial fellow from Beit Shemesh (a small city located one hour southwest of Jerusalem). The man's name was Opher. He informed us that he was a pantomime artist who did mute dramas of the great Bible characters in the Old Testament like Abraham, Isaac, and Jacob. He showed us a presentation on his mini-DVD player. After viewing his reenactment of the Akedah (Abraham offering up his son Isaac), I shared with Opher that this was a Messianic type of Abba God offering up for Israel and the world His one and only unique Son for our sins.

Opher quickly surmised we were believers in Yeshua.

Paul and I affirmed that not only do we believe He is the Messiah but that all of Jesus' first followers were Jewish. I gave him the Gospel tract in Hebrew that gaves a list of all the major prophecies made about Messiah in the Tanach and the corresponding fulfillment by Yeshua in the B'rit Hadashah (the Hebrew phrase for The New Testament).

Opher sat next to Todd on the plane and accepted a Gospel tract in Hebrew. He is a pantomime artist.

Opher wanted to go through some of these prophecies with us. At this point in our conversation, a young Orthodox man from the Chabad movement rudely interrupted our conversation. He had been sitting in the row in front of us.

This man was attempting to discourage and dissuade Opher from hearing the Gospel. The Chabad movement promotes the notion that the late Rabbi Menachem Schneerson of Brooklyn, New York, was the Messiah.

This picture of Schneerson taken in Jerusalem says of Him in Hebrew: "Long live the King and the Messiah."

I bluntly challenged this man and told him in no uncertain terms that all the evidence from Scripture and Jewish history indubitably point to Jesus of Nazareth being the only One who is the Messiah foretold by Moses and the Prophets. The young man claimed that Yeshua could not be the Messiah since His father was not Jewish. By this I assumed that this man was reflecting a tradition of Orthodox Judaism from the Talmud that teaches Jesus' father was a Roman soldier named Pantera who had an illicit relationship with his mother Mary. This was further verified when the man told me to read the Gemara, which is the second part of the Talmud providing commentary and explanation of it. A *pilpul* (a theological debate in Jewish circles) began to develop between this intrusive fellow and me.

My reply was to say that Yeshua's Father was God and His lineage was indeed Jewish on His mother's side. I went on to inform him that Joseph, particularly, could not have been the natural father since he came from King Jeconiah's genealogical line (see *Matthew 1:12*), which God cursed and spoke through the prophet Jeremiah that none of Jeconiah's descendants would ever sit on the throne of David as king of Israel! *"O earth, earth, earth, hear the word of the Lord. Thus says the Lord: 'Write this man down as childless, a man who shall not prosper in his days; for none of his descendants shall prosper, sitting on the throne of David, and ruling Judah anymore"* (Jeremiah 22:29-30). Thus, Joseph, the legal father of Jesus, could not have been the physical father of Jesus because of this curse pronounced on Jeconiah's descendants that would include Joseph and prevent him or his children from reigning on the throne of David as king of Israel. But Jesus was not affected by this curse because his physical Jewish descent came from David through his mother Mary, who conceived him by the supernatural power of the Holy Spirit *(Matt. 1:18; Luke 3:21-38)*.

When asked, the Orthodox man expressed complete ignorance about this key prophecy in *Jeremiah 22:29-30*. So I went on to say that the prophets foretold that the Messiah would be the Son of God and therefore God is His father (see *Psalm 2:6-8; Isaiah 7:14*)!

The Orthodox man angrily expressed his bewilderment over this. I point blank asked him if he had read the evidence for Yeshua being the Messiah, historically written by Jewish eyewitnesses in the New Testament. He smugly answered, "no." I then replied, "You can't very well dismiss something you are ignorant of, nor haven't honestly investigated." After this, the man said nothing more to me. Satan, no doubt, was using his interruption to discourage Opher from investigating these important matters for himself. Nevertheless, Opher accepted a copy of the New Testament in Hebrew and a Gospel tract as well. Pray now that nothing and no one will keep him from coming to faith in the Messiah Jesus.

✝ ✡ ✝ ✡ ✝ ✡ ✝

The first day in Israel was spent overnight in Tel Aviv. The next day we left for Tiberias. Halfway to our destination, the Holy Spirit compelled Paul and me to stop at a national park in northwest Israel called Tel Megiddo. This is an ancient archaeological site that stands on an imposing hill overlooking the Valley of Armageddon. The area is where the future battle of Armageddon will occur between Jesus Christ and His heavenly armies who will defeat the Anti-Christ and the armies of the world *(see Revelation 16:16; 19)*.

Once we arrived at this historical location, the Lord led us to witness to a lady whose name was Esther. She owned a jewelry shop there. Paul and I were able to share with her about the prophetic significance of the future Battle of

Esther, who owned this jewelry shop near Armageddon, had read the Tanach, so Todd recommended that she complete her knowledge by reading the B'rit Hadashah.

Armageddon that will soon take place at that exact location. We shared that the Bible teaches this last battle ending the present age will be Satan's last attempt to remove the Jewish people from the land of Israel so that they will be no more. But Yeshua will return in power and great glory as King of kings and Lord of lords to rescue His Chosen People from annihilation and establish His Kingdom over all the earth *(see Joel 3 and Revelation 19)*. When we learned that Esther had read the Tanach, we suggested that she read the B'rit Hadashah so that she can have a complete knowledge of the Messiah prophesied in the Old Testament and fulfilled in the New.

The Lord then providentially arranged for her brother to be called in so that he could also hear our witness about Messiah Jesus and what Bible prophecy says about the future battle of Armageddon. Esther's brother, Eli, translated for us so that his sister could understand better what we were saying about these various things that concern Israel's role in End-Time Bible prophecy. Both of them received a Hebrew New Testament and Gospel tracts that give a biblical overview of Israel's divine history from the Exodus event to the second coming of the Messiah at the Battle of Armageddon.

Eli, Esther's brother, translated Todd and Paul's witness to her so that she could fully understand the depth of what they said

✝ ✡ ✝ ✡ ✝ ✡ ✝

Next we stopped in the town of Afula. The language barrier proved difficult there and several Israelis were not interested, in engaging in conversation—a rare exception here. At one point, two ladies in a thrift shop said we were "crazy" in their broken English when we attempted to converse with them about Yeshua being the Messiah of Israel—a hazard that comes with this calling.

✝ ✡ ✝ ✡ ✝ ✡ ✝

As we were leaving this little town, Paul felt compelled by the Spirit to stop at a mini-mart. A woman at the counter greeted us with an English, "hello." Paul responded by asking her if she spoke English. She answered in the affirmative. Her son Moshe (Moses) came from the back of the store and asked if he could help us. Paul asked if they sold dried apricots. Such a mundane request opened the door for us to share the Gospel of Yeshua Who as the preeminent descendant of Abraham came to bless the entire world with redemption.

Paul and I shared with Moshe from the Hebrew text of *Genesis 12:1-3* how such a prophecy has been historically fulfilled in the history of the Jewish people and how the Abrahamic seed of blessing is talking about Yeshua the

*Moshe listened to Paul and Todd and accepted
a Messianic Jewish Gospel tract*

Messiah *(see Galatians 3:16)*. He listened attentively and then made a surprise declaration that when a Jewish person blesses a genuine Christian who loves Israel, the former will truly be blessed by the latter—a divine work of mutual reciprocity here. Although Moshe was not open to receiving a free copy of the New Testament in Hebrew, he did accept a Messianic Jewish Gospel tract detailing the historical and biblical evidence for Yeshua being the Messiah.

✞ ✡ ✞ ✡ ✞ ✡ ✞

A few hours after we arrived in the city of Tiberias, we went to the Galilee Experience bookstore to pick up Hebrew Bibles (thanks to Eric Morey and his staff there for faithfully providing Hebrew Bibles to distribute to the Israeli people every time we go to Israel). A Russian shop owner who has a grocery market next to the bookstore motioned us over to look in his shop. We were able to share God's love for the Jewish people with him by using a Russian Gospel tract declaring how much Yeshua loves all of mankind and what He did to prove that love. We left this tract with him and we pray that the Holy Spirit will win his heart over to faith in Yeshua as Savior and Lord.

Todd goes through a Russian Gospel tract with this Russian shop owner

✝ ✡ ✝ ✡ ✝ ✡ ✝

While Paul and I were in Tiberias, we felt compelled to go to the Caesar Hotel. On several prior mission trips, I have done the same thing and God used it for an opportunity to present the Gospel of Jesus the Messiah. This time we ended up conversing with our waitress in the restaurant. Her name was Renanah (which in Hebrew means "happiness.").

Paul and I asked her about the state of tourism in Israel. Renanah said it had picked up some since the relative lull of the intifada. Eventually, our conversation shifted to what God was doing in Israel. On this subject, we mentioned to her that the modern rebirth of the state of Israel with the subsequent return of the Jewish people to their ancient homeland is not only a major fulfillment of End-time Bible prophecy but also a great work of God to prepare them for the return of the Messiah.

The focus of our Gospel witness to Renanah concentrated on the identity of who this Messiah is. When Paul and I told her that Messianic prophecy found in the Jewish Bible

Renanah was very willing to learn about the deity of Jesus

uniquely points to Yeshua of Nazareth being the Messiah of Israel, she replied that in school she was taught that Jesus was no better than a prophet. At this point in the conversation, Paul astutely observed that Jews living in Jesus' day commonly held the same belief of Jesus. To underscore this, we showed her the Hebrew text of *Matthew 16:16-19*. But we also showed her from this same text that Jesus was more than a prophet. He was proclaimed to be the Messiah and Son of God by Jews like Shimon Kepha (Simon Peter).

Renanah said that she was taught and led to believe that Joseph was the physical father of Jesus. We then related to her that the Jewish Bible predicted the Messiah would be divine and the Son of God *(see Psalm 2:6; Isaiah 7:14)*. To that end, Paul and I explained the prophecy about the Messiah's virgin birth made in *Isaiah 7:14*. We noted that the Hebrew word "almah" meaning "young woman" according to rabbinic tradition also can be translated as "virgin." From that, we showed this young lady how that verse was fulfilled by the virgin birth of Jesus mentioned in *Matthew 1:20-22* which states that He was conceived by the power of the Holy Spirit and not by human means. We also noted in the process that Mary and Joseph were engaged at the time, not married; therefore, they would not have physically come together to have Jesus. Thus, the father of Jesus was none other than the God of Israel.

Renanah was amazed at this supernatural and simple explanation from Scripture. She asked us to come back before leaving Tiberias to talk to her more. She was deeply touched when we gave her a complete Hebrew Bible containing the Old and New Testaments so that she could read and study the evidence for herself.

✝ ✧ ✝ ✧ ✝ ✧ ✝

The next day, Paul and I traveled to Qiryat Shimona in extreme northwest Israel to conduct some Gospel witnessing there and follow up on people I had witnessed to before during the Gospel outreach of March 2004. When Paul and I arrived at Qiryat Shimona, we went to a shopping mall to share Yeshua the Messiah with people. While Paul was getting batteries for his camera, I went next door to a shoe store and struck up a conversation with the owner—a man

Armand's shoe store - he didn't want his picture taken

by the name of Armand. I discussed with him about the miraculous restoration of Israel and the evidence from the Tanach that point to Yeshua being the Messiah. He stoutly refused to consider the latter and shockingly admitted that he believed the Tanach but did not need to read it. Armand said this in answer to my challenge that he read the Tanach and New Testament together for himself and weigh the compelling historical evidence for Yeshua being the Messiah. Though he rejected a free copy of the B'rit Hadashah, Armand was open enough to accept a pamphlet about the Messiahship of Jesus of Nazareth.

Readers, pray that such all-important information will pierce Armand's heart and win him over to faith in Israel's crucified Savior.

✝ ✿ ✝ ✿ ✝ ✿ ✝

Continuing our witness in Qiryat Shimona, Paul and I stopped to witness and talk with two Air Force soldiers on the street to discuss the current conditions in Israel and the safety factor of the country. Both soldiers had the same name—Tomer. They said that the nation of Israel must always be on the alert for terrorism and ready for attack since the tiny democratic nation is surrounded by hostile Arab nations who want nothing less than their destruction. We assured them that despite the constant threat of terrorism and being on the verge of war, the God of Israel will protect the Chosen People so that they will never be uprooted or removed from the land again as God promised in *Amos 9:14-15*.

Of course, Israel's final victory over the anti-Semitic nations of the world awaits the return of the Messiah, we said to the soldiers. We left them with Bible literature proving the case for Yeshua being the Messiah of Israel. Pray for these brave defenders of freedom and democracy in the Holy Land, that the God of their ancestors will reveal His Son to their restless hearts.

These Air Force soldiers, both named Tomer,
are always on the alert for terrorism

✟ ✿ ✟ ✿ ✟ ✿ ✟

Next, we revisited Armand, the middle-aged man Robert Cuccia and I visited in March 2004. At that time, Armand received a copy of the B'rit Hadashah. This time he readily greeted us and remembered the fact that we had given him the Bible in Hebrew a year earlier. Armand said he had been reading it continually. When we asked him if he still had a certain Gospel tract I gave him a year earlier, his answer was that he remembered reading it but did not know if he still had a copy of it. At this, Paul and I asked him if he would like another copy. He quickly responded, "Yes." So we gave him another tract sharing the Gospel in a Jewish context.

Armand, to whom Todd and Robert witnessed the previous year, said he had been continually reading the B'rit Hadashah they gave him

✟ ✿ ✟ ✿ ✟ ✿ ✟

An elderly Jewish couple approached us and challengingly asked what we were doing. We said we came to Israel to spread the good news about Israel's long-forgotten Messiah. The elderly couple instinctively knew we were talking about Yeshua. The wife said to Paul that she appreciated the support we showed for Israel, but sternly charged us not to proclaim the message of Yeshua to try and "change the Jews". Paul wisely informed her that our purpose was not to take away Judaism from the Jewish people but to help them realize that it finds its ultimate meaning and fulfillment in Yeshua the Messiah and whoever believes in Him is already Jewish in heart, whether he or she be Jew or Gentile *(see Romans 2:28-29)*.

The woman's husband, Moshe, then made the unsubstantiated claim that the New Testament was not reliable because it was written some 200 years after the alleged events. I quickly retorted that all the Gospel accounts were indeed written by eyewitnesses who had seen and been with Jesus throughout His three and a half years of ministry in Israel. These eyewitness accounts agree in essential details and have proven to be admissible in any court of law by any qualified jurist. All these accounts were written within a generation of the events themselves (covering a period of twenty to sixty years after the events). Furthermore, the risen Messiah was seen by over five hundred eyewitnesses as documented in *I Corinthians 15:1-7*.

Moshe then attempted to claim that when the Messiah comes, He would come to reign over the earth. We said to Moshe that he was confusing the Second Coming for the First Coming. The Messiah had already come to suffer and die for the sins of Israel and the world. He will return in the future to Israel and establish His reign on the earth as the prophets have foretold. Paul and I alluded to *Isaiah 53* as a first coming prophecy that Jesus clearly fulfilled in His sufferings and atoning death. Moshe said that Isaiah was speaking about Israel collectively and not Yeshua or the Messiah. This view is a modern Jewish interpretation of the text in order to avoid the obvious reference to Jesus. But we accurately told him that the majority of the ancient rabbis believed *Isaiah 53* was talking about the suffering Messiah. Therefore, the rabbinic testimony of ancient, biblical Judaism was on our side here.

We ended our friendly but spirited debate with Moshe and his wife by giving them a Messianic Jewish Gospel tract introducing the evidence from Scripture and Jewish history proving that Jesus is the Messiah of Israel. Amazingly, Moshe took it to read and thanked us for our support of the Jewish people.

✝ ✿ ✝ ✿ ✝ ✿ ✝

Returning from Qiryat Shimona, I decided to show Paul the ancient ruins of Capernaum where Peter and some of the apostles lived and where Jesus' home base for ministry was located. As we were leaving from there, two young Israeli women came running up to our car wanting to hitch a ride to Tabgha—the traditional place where Yeshua multiplied the five barley loaves and two fish.

These Jewish girls were hitchhiking (which is common among the young people in Israel proper) to visit each of the historical sites of Jesus' ministry in Galilee. This was simply amazing to hear when you sadly consider that most Jews in Israel will not visit the "holy places" where Yeshua the Messiah taught and performed His miracles. The two girls told us that the rabbis traditionally forbid in the strongest terms their own people from venturing to these important biblical locations.

*These young Jewish girls were visiting each of the historical
sites of Jesus' ministry in Galilee, a thing forbidden by their rabbi*

But the Ruach Hakodesh (Hebrew for the Holy Spirit) of God obviously placed the desire in the hearts of these two girls to visit these Messianic locations where Jesus walked so that Paul and I could powerfully and boldly share with them the life and message of Yeshua the Messiah. The names of the two girls were Hadarah and Ortal. They listened as Paul and I carefully explained to them that the life of Jesus was and is supremely important for the Jewish person to know. His life and divine authority as the God of Israel in human flesh has the absolute power to change lives and determine our eternal destiny *(see John 5:24-30)*.

Ortal and Hadarah listened but suddenly balked when we offered them a Hebrew New Testament, telling us that their rabbis prohibited them from reading it. Both girls placed a high esteem on the opinions of the rabbis who they said would determine when the Messiah comes and Who He would be. They, like so many in modern Israel, have been erroneously taught that Jesus and the New Testament is a Gentile religion that opposes the Jewish people. But we responded by pointing out that the Scriptures, not the rabbis on their own authority, are the only reliable source for identifying the Messiah.

Rabbis have failed of themselves to correctly identify the true Messiah as Jewish history as shown time and time again with the recurrence of false messiahs. Two examples from ancient and modern Judaism were mentioned at this point in our conversation with the two girls. Rabbi Akiva mistakenly proclaimed that Simon Bar Khocbah was the Messiah in 130 A.D. when the latter led the second and last revolt against the Roman Empire and subsequently was shamefully defeated and killed, never to rise again. In our time, we have the Lubavitch movement loudly claiming that their late Rabbi Menachem Schneersohn was the Messiah despite the fact that he fails to have even remotely fulfilled any Messianic prophecies of the Bible.

When we showed them from the B'rit Hadashah that Yeshua was a born and bred Israeli Jew who loved Israel and its people, they were genuinely shocked. Paul and I further shared with them that God gives us free will and therefore the freedom to choose and think for ourselves, unlike most rabbis who control and restrict their people, forbidding them from looking into the New Testament (written from cover to cover by Jews). Besides, we further pointed out to these girls, if they were already visiting places Jesus went, they should logically complete the picture by reading the whole account of His living in Israel as a Torah-observant Jew.

The Holy Spirit used our simple but inescapable logic to convince these two young ladies to reconsider and read the truth about the very Jewish Jesus written by His Jewish followers in the New Testament. Consequently, they received our tracts entitled "Love The Jewish People" and also accepted, at last, a Hebrew translation of the New Testament.

Our sincere prayer is that both Ortal and Hadarah will feel compelled to read this sacred volume and come to the saving revelation God gave Peter in *Matthew 16:16* when saying to Yeshua, ***"You are the Messiah, the Son of the living God."***

✞ ✡ ✞ ✡ ✞ ✡ ✞

While in the Galilee, Paul and I decided to walk the streets of Tiberias and witness to the shop keepers and vendors. This city is one of the ministry's frequent places to conduct witnessing and evangelism among the Jewish and Arab people living there. Paul and I decided to go into a music store that specializes in selling acoustic and electric guitars. Paul is a professional musician and guitar player and wisely used his calling and gift in this area to strike up a conversation with the owner of the music store. The owner was a Russian Jew named Alex who immigrated to Israel several years ago.

After talking to this man at length, we discovered that his religious view was that God is essentially the same no matter what religion. So then Allah, Krishna, and Yahweh are really different names for the same God. I have empirically discovered from my frequent travels to Israel that this is a common view standard among many secular Jews in Israel. We answered Alex by gently, but firmly, explaining to him that the God of Israel is unique and incomparable with any other god without any peer or rival *(see Isaiah 44:6-8, 45: 18-22)*. To prove this, Yahweh foretold long ago Israel's history and has brought it to pass up to the present hour as the Scriptures clearly reveal. He would do this to prove, among other things, that He alone is the one true God and there is no other. No other god of any religion has given prophecy after prophecy and brought it to pass as the God of the Bible has. ***"Remember this, and show yourselves men; Recall to mind, O you transgressors. Remember the former things of old, For I am God, and there is no other; I am God, and there is none like Me, declaring the end from the beginning, and from ancient times things that are not yet done"*** *(see Isaiah 46: 8-10)*. Such a fact that the God of Israel has done this disproves the popular view of religious pluralism. Alex listened and received some biblical literature on this subject detailing how God has revealed Himself through the biblical history of Israel and the Messiah—Yeshua of Nazareth.

Alex is a Russian Jew and owns a music store in Tiberias

✝ ✤ ✝ ✤ ✝ ✤ ✝

Our next witnessing encounter of that day occurred in a video store. Paul and I got into a discussion with the sales lady (her name was Shlomit) about God's failproof method for ascertaining the true identity of the Messiah when He comes to Israel versus the false Messiahs that have and will come. We informed her that this proven method is found in the many Messianic prophecies contained in the Jewish Scriptures (the Tanach). The prophecies that predict the first coming of the Messiah like His birth in Bethlehem *(Micah 5:1-2)* and His ministry beginning in the region of Galilee *(Isaiah 9:1-2)* are just some of the many prophetic events that were fulfilled in the life of Yeshua alone and were a few of the many prophecies that were fulfilled when Yeshua the Messiah came the first time to Israel.

Shlomit expressed simple amazement over this. She told us that she never heard this before. How ironic when you consider that we were standing in the very area Jesus conducted most of His three year ministry; the region of Galilee. Paul and I offered her a free Hebrew Bible that included the New Testament. She could then read and research on her own to learn of the historical record about

Shlomit was happy to receive a copy of the Scriptures so that she could research the Messianic prophecies herself

the Jewish Messiah and how His birth, life, death, and resurrection fulfilled all the prophecies that pertain to the first coming of the Messiah. Shlomit accepted the Scriptures with warm gratitude.

Hopefully, with our prayers joined together for this young lady, she will study and read the Word of God which her own people wrote under the inspiration of God's Spirit. May she learn and personally meet God's Son and Israel's Messiah so that saving faith will resonate within her heart.

✞ ✡ ✞ ✡ ✞ ✡ ✞

Near the end of our stay in Tiberias, we revisited a Jewish woman named Katrina. This was the third year in a row that we ministered to her. Such repeated visits are naturally necessary to build on our continual Gospel witness to her about Yeshua the Messiah. I had met and shared the Gospel with Katrina a year and a half earlier at the tourist center where she works. This time, when I returned to Israel, Paul Colley helped in this follow-up visit.

Katrina seemed to be more open to the message of the Gospel on this visit. But this time her face was long and sad. Katrina said she was down because, in her estimate, conditions in Israel have become more hopeless and desperate with the future being more uncertain. Katrina also added that the world also seemed to her to be increasingly insensitive, materialistic, cold, and more and more hateful in general and particularly toward the Chosen People. The expression of a world-weary disposition on Katrina's part allowed Paul and me to share with her that such moral conditions were foretold by Yeshua and the Apostle Paul in *Matthew 24* and *1 Timothy 3:1-6*, respectively. Indeed, it was here that I pointed out to Katrina that the ancient rabbis of the first century also taught that the world of humanity would universally grow more and more evil and immoral right before the Messiah comes.

The rabbis coined a Hebrew phrase for this time period of great moral declension and apostasy from the one true God.

They called it "Chevlei Hamashiach" (which translated into English means, "the birth pangs of the Messiah"). Katrina said that as a Jew she was familiar with this idea. We said to her, furthermore, that Yeshua described and foretold the same event under the same term of "birth pangs" in *Matthew 24:8*; we were quick to add that there is real hope and deliverance from a moral slide into hopelessness, hate, and despair. The answer is in Yeshua's personal promise of a better world to come when He returns at the Rapture for his bride, the Church, and takes them home to God the Father's glorious house in heaven. We then showed her that wonderful promise the Messiah made to His own in *John 14:1-6*.

Katrina then said that the problem with the world has always been the fact that our hatred for one another has eclipsed and replaced love. Paul and I basically agreed with this simple but sobering assessment and further added that love for God and loving your neighbor as yourself is the warp and woof of God's law. Thus, the only way a person can possibly achieve these two fundamental acts is by having God's law of love inscribed in the heart and lived out by the indwelling presence of the Holy Spirit.

During this third witness to Katrina, she was much more open to hearing about Yeshua the Messiah

To confirm this from the Jewish Scriptures, Paul took the initiative to show Katrina that the God of Israel prophesied this very thing as a part and parcel of the New Covenant He promised to give Israel in *Jeremiah 31:31-33*—**"Behold, the days are coming, says the Lord, when I will make a new covenant with the house of Israel and with the house of Judah—not according to the covenant that I made with their fathers in the day that I took them by the hand to lead them out of the land of Egypt, My covenant which they broke, though I was a husband to them, says the Lord. But this is the covenant that I will make with the house of Israel after those days, says the Lord: I will put My law in their minds, and write it on their hearts; and I will be their God, and they shall be My people."** This can only become a reality by a living trust and indwelling of the One who came and ratified this New Covenant—Yeshua of Nazareth as the inspired writer of the New Testament book Hebrews formally testifies to the Jewish believers in *Hebrews 9-10*.

Katrina read both these passages in Jeremiah and Hebrews and wrote them down in her notebook for further study. I was encouraged by the fact that Katrina is gradually realizing that the answer for the problem of evil does not lie in humanity for the simple fact man is flawed and inherently sinful. She is now open to the possibility that this Messiah we have extensively talked to her about during the last three visits to Israel is the only real and lasting answer for life and death!

✞ ✿ ✞ ✿ ✞ ✿ ✞

Our Gospel witness continued in Tiberias when Paul and I went to a grocery store to purchase some necessities. I felt led to give a Jewish Gospel tract in Hebrew to the security guard who checked our belongings at the entrance (for this is standard procedure for those in Israel fighting to prevent terrorism). When we left the store, the security guard had already read the booklet we gave him. He asked us about our belief in Yeshua being the Messiah, for the tract Paul and I gave him argued the case from Scripture that Jesus is the Messiah of the Jewish people.

The guard's name was Yoav. He wanted to argue that the rabbis like Rabbi Menachem Schneersohn were worthy of more honor and attention. But Paul and I explained to Yoav that Jesus of Nazareth was the only one qualified to receive honor and belief as the Messiah because He alone fulfilled the Messianic prophecies that were foretold by Moses and the Prophets of Israel in the Jewish Scriptures.

Yoav firmly stated that the New Testament was not worthy of the same esteem and belief as the Old Testament due to the New Testament writers' recurring declaration that the Messiah of Israel has come in the Person of Jesus of Nazareth. This to Yoav, and especially the Orthodox which he was, is a great offense and a stumbling stone—as it has been to most of Israel since the time of Jesus.

We then challenged Yoav on this by saying to him that if he was a follower of Moses and the Torah, he would have believed in the Messiah Jesus, of whom Moses clearly wrote about in the Torah *(see Genesis 3:15; Deuteronomy 18:15-19).* Yoav responded to this by reiterating the common belief of

Yoav read the literature given him, but argued that the New Testament could not be held equal to the Old Testament

Orthodox Judaism that there will be two messiahs to come—the suffering Messiah who is called "Messiah, Son of Joseph and the king Messiah, called "Messiah, Son of David" who will conquer and rule when He comes.

Paul and I attempted to explain to him that the rabbis' theory here was biblically erroneous and that the Scriptures actually speak of one Messiah. The Tanach speaks of this same Person as vicariously suffering for the sins of Israel in *Isaiah 53* and later returning in power and great glory to reign over all the earth *(see Isaiah 63)*. The B'rit Hadashah (New Testament) historically records this to be fulfilled in the life of Jesus of Nazareth. Although Yoav adamantly refused to receive a free copy of the New Testament in Hebrew due to the rabbis' paranoid prohibition and disinformation, which he sadly but blindly followed, he did read what we gave him in the form of a Gospel tract that prompted our conversation with Yoav and planted a Gospel seed in his spirit and mind.

✝ ✡ ✝ ✡ ✝ ✡ ✝

Paul and I returned to our hotel that evening. Before going up to our room, we stopped in the lounge to have a cappuccino. The waitress who served us was a young lady whose name was Anat. When engaging in conversation with her, I pointed out the broad bay window in front of us and said to her that much of Yeshua the Messiah's ministry was done in and around the lake of Galilee. She mistook the name of Yeshua to be the Joshua of Moses' time. But I corrected her by saying that it was Yeshua of Nazareth I was talking about. Anat was genuinely surprised and exclaimed she had never known that.

Paul and I then shared with her about the importance of the life of Yeshua for Israel and the world. Indeed we said to her that He was the One that put an unquenchable love for the Jewish people in our hearts. This occurred after He saved us and replaced our hatred and bitterness with His love. She replied that she believed in Elohim, and Yeshua was only good for us. Paul and I then said that to trust in the Messiah is the same as believing in God Himself and that all of us need the Lord's "hesed" (Hebrew for divine grace) to live and be forgiven of sin. She saw the need for this. This grace was supremely given when the God of Israel sent us His Son—Jesus of Nazareth.

Paul and I then offered Anat an opportunity to find this saving grace by reading about the life of Jesus in the New Testament where so many of the events occurred in the region of the Galilee where she lived! Anat was moved by our Gospel witness and accepted a Hebrew copy of the New Testament Scriptures. She thanked us for sharing this love to the Jewish people.

Anat, who lives in the Galilee, was unaware of the historical and miraculous events that took place there

✝ ✿ ✝ ✿ ✝ ✿ ✝

While Paul and I were in Tiberias, we had a chance to stop and visit our Arab friend Eli—the young man Robert

Cuccia and I visited and eventually led to the Lord Jesus over a year ago. Eli was exceedingly glad to see us and I am further happy to report that not only did he recall the exact date of his salvation when Robert and I led him to the Lord, but also amazingly he relayed to us that he was being currently discipled by a pastor and prominent messianic leader of that area whom we had recommended to him a year ago. Praise the Lord Jesus; the Word of God is taking root in Eli's life and bearing fruit showing, indeed, that the work of salvation has taken a firm hold of his life—for that is what this ministry in Israel is all about.

Eli is being discipled by a pastor and prominent messianic leader of the area

✝ ✿ ✝ ✿ ✝ ✿ ✝

Every Gospel outreach I conduct in Israel, I always endeavor to take one day out to make the arduous drive to Mount Hermon to talk to the IDF (Israeli Defense Forces) soldiers stationed there about the Gospel of the Jewish Messiah and to encourage them for protecting Israel's democracy against terrorist incursions from Syria and the hostile Arab nations surrounding them. The Mount Hermon

range is the farthest point in the northeastern border of Israel. Mount Hermon defines the borders between Israel and Syria. Israel defeated Syria in the Six Day War when Syria unwisely invaded Israel without the slightest provocation along with other Arab nations for the express purpose of wiping the Jewish State off the map.

Israel defeated Syria along with the rest of the Arab invaders and captured the Golan Heights with part of Mount Hermon. Occupying the Golan Heights is crucial for Israel today. This area is the strategic high ground giving them the vantage point in defending themselves against any future attack from Syria. Before Israel acquired the Golan Heights, Syria regularly fired deadly missiles into Israel injuring and killing Jews who were living in the lower Galilee region.

When Paul and I reached the military checkpoint leading up to the military base at the top of Mount Hermon, we were able to talk to the three IDF soldiers. Two of these soldiers were both named Alex. Paul and I stated to them that their expert skills in fighting terrorism have been an excellent form of training for the American armed forces fighting terrorism in Afghanistan and Iraq.

We further shared with these IDF soldiers that we came to Israel to personally thank the Jewish people for obeying God's call to bring His Word and the Savior to the world. At this, the soldiers looked both startled and amazed that people like Paul and me would come to Israel and make the lengthy drive up to Mount Hermon just to share this. We also said that in order to discharge our spiritual debt to the Jewish people, we come to Israel to give back what they have given to us—that would be the New Testament of Jesus the Messiah, the greatest Jew who ever lived. We boldly spoke to them about God's plan for them as fulfilled in Yeshua the Messiah.

The soldiers gladly received a Hebrew New Testament (B'rit Hadashah) and Messianic Gospel tracts showing how a Jewish person can receive Yeshua as the Messiah.

Like the IDF, we too are on a mission as soldiers for Jesus in a spiritual army carrying His message of love back to the people and place it came from.

And the mission continues... ✝

¹ For Zion's sake I will not hold My peace,
And for Jerusalem's sake I will not rest,
Until her righteousness goes forth as
brightness,
And her salvation as a lamp that burns.
² The Gentiles shall see your righteousness,
And all kings your glory.
You shall be called by a new name,
Which the mouth of the LORD will name.
³ You shall also be a crown of glory
In the hand of the LORD,
And a royal diadem
In the hand of your God.
⁴ You shall no longer be termed Forsaken,
Nor shall your land any more be termed
Desolate; But you shall be called
Hephzibah, and your land Beulah;
For the LORD delights in you,
And your land shall be married.
⁵ For as a young man marries a virgin,
So shall your sons marry you;
And as the bridegroom rejoices over the
bride, So shall your God rejoice over you.

Isaiah 62:1-5

B'rit Hadashah is a non-profit ministry dedicated to full-time evangelism to the nation of Israel. This is a mandate by God, carried out by the Spirit of the Lord Jesus Christ.

To do this takes financial support from Christians who love the Jews and want to bless Israel with an opportunity for them to be saved by hearing and believing the Gospel. I can tell you from personal experience the Jewish people are open and willing to listen about why Jesus is the Messiah of Israel and the world.

The only way I can carry out this last-days Gospel outreach to Israel is if people like you obey the Holy Spirit's leading and give to this ministry. For **"How then shall they call on Him in whom they have not believed? And how shall they believe in Him whom they have not heard? And how shall they hear without a preacher? And how shall they preach unless they are sent"** (Romans 10:14).

What greater blessing to give to the Jewish people than to afford them the opportunity to hear the Gospel and believe it for salvation. God promises a special blessing on those who bless the Chosen People. In Genesis 12:3, the Lord says, **"I will bless those who bless you."** As you give into this ministry, God will bless you, **"not that I seek a gift, but I seek the fruit that abounds to your account"** (Phil. 4:17). To support this ministry, and to sign up for our free monthly newsletter, visit our website:

www.SearchTheScripturesOnline.org
or
www.Brit-Hadashah.org

or send your tax deductible donations to:
B'rit Hadashah Ministries
P.O. Box 796127
Dallas, Texas 75379-6127

Donations are tax deductible in the U.S. as you give to this 501(c)(3) Non-profit ministry. **May our God, the God of Israel, abundantly bless those who partner with us in this great end-time commission.**

Dr. Todd Baker
President/Founder

Sign up for your free subscription to
our monthly newsletter at
www.SearchTheScripturesOnline.org
or
www.Brit-Hadashah.org

Printed in the United States
70181LV00005B/1-9

9 781600 343988